17

LD TESTAMENT

COLLEGEVILLE BIBLE COMMENTARY

MW01038215

JOEL, OBADIAH, HAGGAI, ZECHARIAH, MALACHI

Mary Margaret Pazdan, O.P.

THE LITURGICAL PRESS

Collegeville, Minnesota

ABBREVIATIONS

Gen—Genesis	Eccl—Ecclesiastes	John—John
Exod—Exodus	Song—Song of Songs	Acts—Acts
Lev—Leviticus	Wis—Wisdom	Rom—Romans
Num—Numbers	Sir—Sirach	1 Cor—1 Corinthians
Deut—Deuteronomy	Isa—Isaiah	2 Cor—2 Corinthians
Josh—Joshua	Jer—Jeremiah	Gal—Galatians
Judg—Judges	Lam—Lamentations	Eph—Ephesians
Ruth—Ruth	Bar—Baruch	Phil—Philippians
1 Sam—1 Samuel	Ezek—Ezekiel	Col—Colossians
2 Sam—2 Samuel	Dan—Daniel	1 Thess—1 Thessalonians
1 Kgs—1 Kings	Hos—Hosea	2 Thess—2 Thessalonians
2 Kgs—2 Kings	Joel—Joel	1 Tim—1 Timothy
1 Chr—1 Chronicles	Amos—Amos	2 Tim—2 Timothy
2 Chr—2 Chronicles	Obad—Obadiah	Titus—Titus
Ezra—Ezra	Jonah—Jonah	Phlm—Philemon
Neh—Nehemiah	Mic—Micah	Heb—Hebrews
Tob—Tobit	Nah—Nahum	Jas—James
Jdt—Judith	Hab—Habakkuk	1 Pet—1 Peter
Esth—Esther	Zeph—Zephaniah	2 Pet—2 Peter
1 Macc—1 Maccabees	Hag—Haggai	1 John—1 John
2 Macc—2 Maccabees	Zech—Zechariah	2 John—2 John
Job—Job	Mal—Malachi	3 John—3 John
Ps(s)—Psalm(s)	Matt—Matthew	Jude—Jude
Prov—Proverbs	Mark—Mark	Rev—Revelation
	Luke—Luke	

Nihil obstat: Robert C. Harren, J.C.L., *Censor deputatus.*

Imprimatur: ✛ George H. Speltz, D.D., Bishop of St. Cloud. January 16, 1986.

The text of the Books of Joel, Obadiah, Haggai, Zechariah, and Malachi from the NEW AMERICAN BIBLE, copyright © 1970 by the Confraternity of Christian Doctrine, Washington, D.C., is reproduced herein by license of said copyright owner. No part of the NEW AMERICAN BIBLE may be reproduced in any form without permission in writing. All rights reserved.

ISBN 0-8146-1424-8 (volume 17 O.T.); ISBN 0-8146-1394-2 (complete set O.T.)

Library of Congress Cataloging in Publication Data
Pazdan, Mary Margaret, 1942–

Joel, Obadiah, Haggai, Zechariah, Malachi.

(Collegeville Bible commentary. Old Testament ; 17)
Includes the texts of Joel, Obadiah, etc., from the New American Bible.
1. Bible. O.T. Minor Prophets—Commentaries. I. Bible. O.T. Joel. English. New American. 1986. II. Bible. O.T. Obadiah. English. New American. 1986. III. Bible. O.T. Haggai. English. New American. 1986. IV. Bible. O.T. Zechariah. English. New American. 1986. V. Bible. O.T. Malachi. English. New American. 1986. VI. Title. VII. Series.
BS1560.P39   1986   224'.9   86-7281
ISBN 0-8146-1424-8 (pbk.)

Cover: "The pomegranate, the date palm also, and the apple, all the trees of the field are dried up" (Joel 1:12). *Photo:* Date palm tree *by Richard T. Nowitz.*

CONTENTS

The Books of Joel, Obadiah, Haggai, Zechariah, and Malachi

Introduction

A variety of starting points is available for exploring a text of the Bible. The process of selection is similar to how a viewer encounters snapshots in a photo album. One individual focuses sharply on a single image, while another admires the arrangements or qualities of composition. A third person enjoys the sequence and patterning of several pages, whereas a fourth examines an entire album for imaginative contours. If the snapshots or the album captures the attention of the viewer, they may provide opportunities for additional variations by repeated inspection.

The viewer's experiences also inform what is perceived. A family member, relative, or friend is delighted to find memories suddenly revitalized by significant photos that celebrate life (for example, birthdays, anniversaries, summer holidays). Juxtaposed to these photos, however, are others that remind the viewer of circumstances that have modified the moment captured on film (for example, distance, aging, death). Viewers unfamiliar with the photos need explanations from others to give the photo meaning.

The photographer's experiences direct the selection of the subject. Often the photo represents more possibilities to the viewers than the photographer saw in framing the subject. The understanding of the photo deepens when the viewer and the photographer discuss its importance. The reality of the photo is seldom exhausted, because each viewer sees with limited perception.

Like the viewer and photographer, a number of biblical scholars began to dialogue with persons of other academic disciplines. No longer confined to the historical-critical method of the nineteenth century, commentators cautiously applied the distinctive methods of new literary, canonical, and sociological criticism to broaden the possibilities of interpreting prophecy, including the five books treated in this commentary. The interdisciplinary method indicated in scholarly and popular articles for over a decade may provide insights into the meaning of postexilic prophecy, which had been generalized and undervalued.

Why does prophecy from its early development (about 1000 B.C.E.) through the period of the Exile (586–538 B.C.E.) receive more attention in surveys of the Old Testament?

a) The books that record the growth of prophecy are wonderful litera-ture. Nathan, the court prophet, indicts King David (1000–967 B.C.E.) by means of the parable of the ewe lamb (2 Sam 12:1-15). A cycle of narratives about northern Israel (869–815 B.C.E.) records the adventures of Elijah and Elisha: a contest on Mount Carmel with the prophets of Baal, meeting Jeze-bel, miracles, experiences of God, involvement with political and religious leaders (see 1 Kgs 17–21; 2 Kgs 1–9).

Prophetic books named for individuals follow the *narratives about* proph-ets. They offer biographical details, dramatic gestures, and bold prophetic oracles to communicate the word of God. Isaiah, Jeremiah, and Ezekiel ap-pear as inspiring, heroic figures in the struggles of Judah (782–586 B.C.E.). The prophets stimulate interest and imagination for scholars. Concurrently, they appeal to children and adults in catechetical and sermon contexts as well as by their association with literature, music, and art.

b) Many events described by the texts are supported by the parallel liter-ature of the ancient Near East. Archeological data confirms the historical and literary perspectives of preexilic and exilic prophecy. Analysis and com-parison with extrabiblical materials generate additional study and discovery.

c) The books indicate common political-religious dimensions of kingship and temple. Fidelity of the king and community to the Jerusalem temple is *the* standard by which northern Israel and Judah are judged (see 1 Kgs 12–2 Kgs 25). The prophets exhort the people to be faithful to the covenant stipu-lations first formed with God on Mount Sinai through Moses. They develop the ethical dimensions of Torah, images of God and future liberation, often invoking images from Exodus.

d) New Testament authors frequently refer to persons and passages from preexilic and exilic prophecy to describe Jesus, the Jews, and early commu-nities of believers.

When earlier scholars compared postexilic prophecy with the characteris-tics of preexilic and exilic prophecy mentioned above, the former appeared unimportant and secondary in the prophetic corpus. The narratives are lim-ited, lacking in personal detail, and seldom the subject of art or literature. The historical and literary data is sparse; often reconstruction is contradic-tory. The political, social, and religious conditions after the Exile do not com-pare favorably with the symbolic unity of kingship and temple. The texts are quoted infrequently by New Testament authors.

Contemporary scholars do not judge postexilic prophecy by earlier prophecy. Prophetic forms and content aligned to king and temple are no longer considered necessarily normative or significant. What, then, is ap-propriate for interpreting postexilic writings? In this commentary the cen-tral focus is the particular contribution of each book as a witness to restoration after the experience of exile. Information about a particular author, dating, and composition, together with an outline of the book, is given just before the commentary on each book. Considerations common to Joel, Obadiah, Haggai, Zechariah, and Malachi are described below.

Location in the Old Testament

The Jewish canon and the Alexandrian canon include the Books of Joel, Obadiah, Haggai, Zechariah, and Malachi among the Twelve Minor Prophets. What does the division imply? The designation "minor" has been interpreted as meaning "inferior" or "less important," because the Twelve Minor Prophets follow the Latter Prophets (Isaiah, Jeremiah, Ezekiel) in the Jewish canon, and the Prophets (Isaiah, Jeremiah, Baruch, Lamentations, Ezekiel, Daniel) in the Alexandrian canon. The term "minor" probably refers to the size of the texts compared with the prophetic books that precede them.

In a manner unlike that of the Major Prophets, the historical factors for ordering and collecting the Twelve Minor Prophets remain obscure. Scholars examine the canons and the books for implications of how the process may have occurred. In comparing the canons, the first and the seventh through the twelfth books are identical (Hosea, Nahum, Habakkuk, Zephaniah, Haggai, Zechariah, Malachi), while the second through the sixth books are in different order: Jewish canon (Joel, Amos, Obadiah, Jonah, Micah); Alexandrian canon (Amos, Micah, Joel, Obadiah, Jonah).

Which list is earlier? What accounts for the change of order? There are three suggestions for the ordering of the books in each canon: (a) chronology; (b) repetition of words and phrases between books, for example Amos 1:2 and Joel 4:16; (c) mechanical considerations, for example the length of a scroll. Today the questions and suggestions are unresolved.

How twelve independent prophetic books became a collection that was considered as one book is a puzzle. Often the fact that the Twelve could be written on one scroll is given as a solution. Historically, the process of collection was completed by 300 B.C.E. Sirach, writing a century later, acknowledges the prophets in his praise of Israel's heroes:

Then, too, the TWELVE PROPHETS—
may their bones return to life from their resting place!—
Gave new strength to Jacob
and saved him by their faith and hope (Sir 49:10).

Sirach's grandson, translating the Hebrew text into Greek after 132 B.C.E., includes the division of prophets in his foreword: "Many important truths have been handed down to us through the law, the prophets, and the latter authors; and for these the instruction and wisdom of Israel merit praise."

The Minor Prophets were also important to the Qumran community, whose scrolls include a commentary on Micah as well as eight incomplete copies of the Twelve Minor Prophets. In Christian tradition the title "Minor Prophets" is attributed to Augustine (*De civitate Dei*, XVIII, 29). Canonical critics observe that the process of ordering and collecting the Twelve Minor Prophets is less important than the factors involved in shaping each book and the way the final form of each book functioned in a particular community of faith.

Historical background

The ministry and textual tradition of Joel, Obadiah, Haggai, Zechariah, and Malachi extended over two centuries of postexilic Judaism. Although the period is poorly documented, some biblical witness and archeological data are available to reconstruct the historical context for the prophets and their literary records.

2 Kgs 23:36–25:30, 2 Chr 36:9-21, and Jer 32–34; 37–39; 52 interpret the final days of Judah and the deportations to Babylon. In 599 B.C.E. King Jehoiakim refused to pay tribute money to Nebuchadnezzar, ruler of the neo-Babylonian empire. Although the biblical texts are unclear about Jehoiakim's fate, they indicate that his son Jehoiachin had ruled for only three months when Nebuchadnezzar forced him to surrender Jerusalem in the spring of 597 B.C.E. Jehoiachin, the royal household, craftspersons, military officials, and prominent citizens were sent into captivity. The sacred vessels of the temple were also transported to Babylon.

To reduce the possibility of further rebellion, Nebuchadnezzar appointed Jehoiachin's uncle Zedekiah as king of Judah. For eleven years he wavered between the patronage of the pro-Egyptian party and the protection of Jeremiah. Having chosen resistance as his brother did, he, too, had to surrender to Nebuchadnezzar, who ordered the palace, the temple, and the city destroyed; the ruler and inhabitants were deported to Babylon in 586 B.C.E.

For the few persons remaining near Jerusalem, Nebuchadnezzar appointed Gedaliah as governor. After he was assassinated by a rebel, the Babylonian policy of deportation and division of the land continued in Judah and other parts of the empire. The Edomites, ancient enemies of Israel, seized some territory in Judah. The Book of Obadiah is directed against their treachery. The Book of Lamentations reflects the anguish and tragedy of this period for the Jews.

After Nebuchadnezzar died in 562 B.C.E., the empire gradually declined and Cyrus the Persian seized the opportunity for twenty years of conquest. His success culminated in the surrender of Babylon in 539 B.C.E. Cyrus' liberal attitude toward subject peoples extended to authorizing their return and financing the restoration of temples and cults. The Cyrus Cylinder, an inscription written on a clay barrel and telling of Cyrus' Babylonian triumph and of his policy of allowing captives to return to their homelands, indicates his intentions: "May all the gods whom I have placed within their sanctuaries address a daily prayer in my favor . . . that my days may be long."

Cyrus also issued a decree to the Babylonian Jews. Under the leadership of Sheshbazzar, prince of Judah, a small group returned bringing donations from their neighbors and the confiscated temple vessels (Ezra 1:2–2:70). Meanwhile, large numbers remained in Babylon, preferring their homes, structures of community life, and loyalty toward the lenient government to an uncertain future in ravaged Judah (compare Jer 29:1-9).

The returnees found a decimated land, inhospitable landowners, intermarriage, and syncretistic worship. Sheshbazzar, appointed governor, initiated attempts to restore the sacrificial altar and the foundations of the temple. The confused chronology and narrative detail of Ezra, the only biblical record for the period, do not indicate what happened to Sheshbazzar.

After Cyrus' death, Cambyses, his son, reigned until 522 B.C.E. At his death widespread rebellion occurred in many areas of the empire. Darius, an officer of Cambyses' army, stabilized the empire after two years of fierce battles. During that time another group of Babylonian Jews returned to Jerusalem, including Zerubbabel, appointed governor, and Joshua, the high priest. During their dual leadership there were renewed efforts to rebuild the temple.

Obstacles, however, continued to impede progress. Within the community, antagonism over property claims continued. Droughts and poor soil added to the burden of harsh living conditions. Opposition to the restoration came from neighboring areas under Persian control as well as from the Samaritans to the north. Darius intervened to settle the disputed authorization for rebuilding the temple. Haggai and Zechariah, too, encouraged the residents to persevere in their efforts.

In the spring of 515, nearly twenty-five years after Cyrus' decree, the community offered sacrifice to God and dedicated the temple (Ezra 3–6). There is no evaluation of Zerubbabel's leadership. He, like Sheshbazzar, disappeared mysteriously from the narrative of Ezra. Joshua and the priestly class associated with the temple presumably became the source of political and religious authority for the community.

There is a gap of fifty years in the biblical record, although the undated text of Malachi offers an assessment of community life just before the arrival of Ezra. The author condemns the irresponsibility of the priests in cultic matters, intermarriages with non-Jews, and social injustice.

Ezra, commissioned by Artaxerxes I, initiated a religious reform in 458 B.C.E. by condemning intermarriage, appointing honest magistrates and judges, and assembling the people for the reading of the law (Ezra 7:1-10:16; Neh 8:1-9:37). Nehemiah, cupbearer to Artaxerxes I, was governor of Judah from 445-433 B.C.E. He protected Jerusalem from its enemies by supervising the rebuilding of the city walls. After a brief absence, Nehemiah returned as governor (430-418 B.C.E.) to enforce religious laws regarding the support of temple officials, marriage, and observance of the sabbath (Neh 1:1-7:5; 11:1-13:31).

The undated Book of Joel is considered a witness to the situation of the community after the reforms of Ezra and Nehemiah. The author exhorts the people to public prayer and penance to avert God's judgment. It is a preparation for "the day of the Lord," the ultimate judgment between Israel and the nations.

There is a gap of nearly a century in the biblical record, during which time the Persian empire declined and the Greek empire developed under the leadership of Alexander the Great (336-323 B.C.E.). Second Zechariah (chs. 9-14) is addressed to the Jewish community during this emergence of a new world empire. The oracles describe a cosmic battle, the Messiah, and the new kingdom of God.

Attitudes and perspectives about reconstruction

The Babylonian Jews who returned to Jerusalem in two stages participated in the multiple tasks of reconstruction. What challenges did they encounter together with the group already well established in Judah during the Exile? In addition to the obstacles mentioned above, both groups were confronted with the complex question of identity.

The province of Judah was one of several provinces included in the satrapy "West of Euphrates" (see Ezra 4:17, 20; 5:6), whose administrator, the satrap, probably resided in Damascus. Judah enjoyed the type of independence granted to members of the nearly two dozen satrapies of the vast Persian empire, including freedom for cultic activity. Judah, with Jerusalem as its center, can be identified as a temple-community like others restored and subsidized by the central government. Jerusalem functioned both as a cultic center for prayer as well as an administrative center for the province.

The officials appointed by the central government mediated their authority as governors—for example, Sheshbazzar, Zerubbabel, Nehemiah. In daily affairs, however, the priests exercised authority over the community. They decided on the status of individuals in the community according to their participation in and support of the cult. Their legislation about the standards of purity necessary for worshipers included the condemnation of those who engaged in syncretistic worship, those who married resident aliens, and those who transacted business with non-Jews.

Both residents and returnees were affected by these criteria. Tension developed among the two groups, including the priestly class. The conflict among the priestly functionaries resulted in a division of responsibility. The Zadokite priests (returnees from Babylon) assumed the major position for cult and administration; the Levites were relegated to minor positions with little authority.

Some scholars suggest that two mainstreams of religious authority developed from this situation and that this accounts for the decline of prophecy. The theocratic group was associated with the Zadokite priests and the rebuilding of the temple and the reconstitution of religious life according to the Torah and the vision of Ezekiel (Ezek 40–48). The apocalyptic group was associated with the Levites and a future transformation of the present situation according to the vision of Deutero-Isaiah (Isa 40–55). This assessment, however, is too sharp. It does not allow for the plurality of religious experience and perspective.

The manner of restoration of the community and its identity is related to the interpretation of God's revelation as understood by the individual prophet. Each responded to the needs of a particular community. Each had a provisional proclamation directed toward encouraging that community to be faithful to God:

a) *Obadiah* implored God to destroy the Edomites and to vindicate Israel from their deceit.

b) *Haggai* and *Zechariah* believed that the restoration of the temple would hasten the advent of God for the purpose of dwelling in Jerusalem forever. Zechariah also considered the relationship of God to other nations. Both prophets encountered the resistance of the Jerusalemites due to shattered dreams and oppressive living conditions, which curtailed enthusiasm and stamina for reconstruction. Neither prophet was certain about the role of the governors and the priestly class. Even after the completion of the temple, the past could not be an appropriate model for the present.

The ministry of these prophets was effective because they provided inspiration for a common identity among the residents, that is, a temple-community and the reestablished locus for cultic activity. After their deaths the dilemma of unfulfilled prophecy and unresolved relationships among their neighbors continued. Uncertainty, confusion, and instability characterized the period.

c) *Malachi* addressed abuses in cultic practices. *Joel* admonished the community about its relationship to God and its symbolic expression in worship. Both prophets desired a renewal of dedicated religious life for persons who would accept their message.

d) The writings of *Second Zechariah* stirred dormant hope and dispelled the apathy of the community through visions of climactic struggle followed by the day of the Lord, a day when a kingdom of peace and blessing would be secured forever.

These five prophets may well be remembered for activity during a bleak period of Israel's history. Each prophet with his literary record witnesses to a particular situation somewhat influenced by imperial Persian and Greek policies, yet transcending them with a religious vision related to the experience of the community to whom the message is addressed. Being convinced of the fidelity of God, they spoke a message calling the community to respond appropriately. They exhorted the community to be faithful to God, the constant reality of their past history and their present experience.

The postexilic prophets in this series cannot be judged by whether or not their message was fulfilled in subsequent history. The mystery of the faithful God and the manner in which the individual and the community respond are the perspectives that these books develop. In addition, the fact that communities of believers preserved and edited these proclamations and considered them to be the authentic revelation of God indicates their significance for developing faith in postexilic communities.

Literary Forms

The Books of Joel, Obadiah, Haggai, Zechariah, and Malachi contain poetry and prose. There are visions and oracles attributed to the prophets whose names are the superscriptions for the books as well as editorial insertions to consolidate the material and provide interpretation for later communities. The books refer to earlier Scripture (Torah and Prophets) by allusion to and repetition of events and ideas. Occasionally there are direct quotations from earlier prophets.

The literary structure of each book is developed from the particular context in which the message was first proclaimed. Prophetic formulas common to preexilic and exilic books are sometimes located in the postexilic compositions; occasionally they are combined with new patterns. In particular, scholars often regard sections of these books as indicating a new literary form, viewpoint, and content known as "apocalyptic." Since the literary structure of a particular text is a primary indicator for its religious meaning, it is important to understand the structure in order to interpret the significance of the text. A few literary considerations for each book are presented below according to the chronological order already suggested.

Obadiah, the shortest book in the Old Testament, consists of two sets of oracles received in a vision according to the tradition of Jerusalemite prophets. The first set of oracles describes the destruction of Edom (vv. 2-9) in language similar to that of Jer 49:7-22. This neighbor of Israel is condemned for its betrayal of Jerusalem to Babylon (vv. 10-14). The second set was added later to include the day of the Lord as a judgment for all nations (vv. 15-16). The event culminates in the restoration of Israel and the establishment of the universal kingdom of God (vv. 17-21). Some scholars suggest that the structure of the oracles (vv. 2-17) indicates a community at worship proclaiming God's sovereignty through the proclamation of oracles against its enemies.

The two chapters of *Haggai* also contain oracles interspersed with editorial frameworks to interpret them. The frameworks include: (a) the chronology of Haggai's ministry to the residents of Jerusalem (1:1, 15; 2:1, 10, 20); (b) insertions of traditional prophetic formulas to introduce an oracle, such as "the words of the Lord through the prophet . . ." (1:1, 3; 2:1, 10, 20; compare 1:12, 13); (c) a report about the result of Haggai's preaching to the community (1:12, 14). Although words of comfort are included in the oracles, suggesting the judgment of salvation characteristic of classical prophecy (1:13; 2:4, 5), the oracles add a new development—the disputation. Some indications of this pattern are rhetorical questions (1:4; 2:3, 16) and a question-and-answer format (1:9-11).

Oracles do not function as the major literary form of revelation in *First Zechariah* (chs. 1-8); rather, they are a secondary pattern occurring in a collection (chs. 7-8) and attached to visions, which are the primary pattern of revelation (1:7-6:8). The visions constitute some of the most difficult texts to interpret in biblical literature. Some scholars suggest that the significance of the "night" visions consists in providing an alternative to the oracles and visions of Ezekiel (chs. 40-48) and of Haggai about temple reconstruction. Zechariah constructed a theological perspective for fidelity to God in the new situation of "in betweenness."

In the Book of *Malachi* the question-and-answer format that appeared in Haggai (and First Zechariah) becomes the basic structure of the oracles. This catechetical pattern was suitable for exhorting the community and its cult officials to be responsible for their relationships to God. They were urged to revitalize indifferent cultic practices and to observe the laws of marriage and the prohibitions against divorce (1:2-3:21). The two appendices (3:22-24) conclude with an instruction to be faithful to the law and a description of Elijah, God's messenger who will reconcile family members.

The Book of *Joel* is a collection of oracles with two interrelated themes: devastation and salvation. In the first part (1:1-2:17), the prophet functions as a cult figure. He calls the people to repentance in a communal lamentation liturgy intended to avert a disaster far worse than the locust plague. After introducing the concept of "the day of the Lord," Joel admonishes them about their expectations. In the second part (2:18-4:21), the prophet describes the day of the Lord in more detail. Throughout the oracles there is frequent allusion to, or direct quotations of, sayings found in other prophetic collections; for example, Isa 13:6 and Ezek 30:2-3 (Joel 1:15); Zeph 1:14-15 (Joel 2:1-2); Obad 17 (Joel 3:5).

Second Zechariah (chs. 9–14) is separated from First Zechariah by nearly two centuries of political and religious history. The chapters are divided into two sections. Each section has its own introduction (chs. 9–11 and 12–14). Unlike First Zechariah, the oracular structure is prominent. Within the oracles there is no original revelation; rather, the function of the oracles is to collect the expectations of earlier prophets and to indicate how they may be fulfilled; for example, Zeph 3:14ff. (Zech 9:9); Isa 5:26 (Zech 10:8); Joel 4 (Zech 14). Another major difference is the absence of any mention of the temple builders and officials. In addition, there are no chronological indications nor any coherent "historical" framework. Finally, the chapters of Second Zechariah have been assessed for apocalyptic language and viewpoint.

Relationship to apocalyptic writings

In the past fifteen years there has been renewed interest in the origin, language, structure, content, and interpretation of Jewish apocalyptic writings. Postexilic prophecy has been considered a possible source for apocalyptic, since the phenomenon did not parallel the structure and content of classical prophecy. Some scholars constructed a polarity between the "traditionalists" and the "visionaries" existing in the temple-community. Their conflict of interests resulted in the formation of two distinctive groups. The "traditionalists" reaffirmed the position of supporting the temple and its officials. The "visionaries" expressed their radical hopes for a new identity by the transformation of the present situation. Today interdisciplinary analysis with the social sciences, especially cultural anthropology, appears to support this interpretation.

Intra-group conflict and fluctuating circumstances can be catalysts for the formation of apocalyptic groups. The more difficult question is not why *an* apocalyptic viewpoint and literature emerged but why *this particular form* emerged. The religious diversity apparent in postexilic communities suggests that apocalyptic development was not the inevitable result of particular social circumstances.

Most of the present century of scholarship has considered the related question of the origins of apocalyptic language. Did it emerge from prophecy? Is it an adaptation of Persian dualism? Is wisdom literature the matrix? The search for sources appears to be misdirected, since any apocalyptic text combines allusions from a wide range of sources. The meaning of any text is dependent on the sources as well as on the way the sources are combined through the editorial process.

Current investigations of the structure and content of Jewish apocalyptic writings have indicated that some sections of the postexilic prophetic books may be categorized as proto-apocalyptic, for instance, Second Zechariah, Joel 3–4; Mal 3–4. Sharing a few structural similarities and features of content, however, does not indicate that some postexilic texts can be interpreted according to apocalyptic world views. The decision to investigate the linguistic affinity and structural parallel of postexilic prophecy to apocalyptic literature underscores the reluctance of some scholars to analyze these prophetic texts for their own contributions.

The Book of Joel

Introduction

Authorship

What is known about the author of this book is limited to 1:1, which names and identifies him: "The word of the Lord which came to Joel, son of Pethuel." The verse uses a traditional prophetic formula, "the word of the Lord came to . . . ." The name Joel means "Yahweh is God." It is recorded by the Chronicler (see 1 Chr 4:35; 5:4; 7:3; 11:38; Ezra 10:43; Neh 11:9), whose texts were compiled in the postexilic period. Pethuel is mentioned nowhere else in the Old Testament. "Joel ben Pethuel" may designate the author of the book.

Other biographical detail is inferred from the text. Many scholars suggest that Joel was a cult prophet attached to the Jerusalem temple-community. His concern for temple worship and his prophecies in liturgical form may indicate that he was a temple official. He never identified himself, however, as a priest.

Dating of the text

The superscription of the book indicates no chronological setting for Joel. Earlier scholars, however, suggested a preexilic period for the book, noting its position in the Jewish canon between Hosea and Amos, and its repetition of words and phrases from Amos (compare Joel 4:18 and Amos 9:13). Although a minority of scholars still favor a preexilic dating, the majority of them locate Joel in the Persian period. The book suggests some literary dependency of Joel on earlier prophetic traditions (see pp. 13–14). Historical allusions (1:9; 4:6), the absence of earlier administrators (kings and governors), and the lack of internal dissension and internal oppression also imply a late postexilic period. The approximate dating of the text is 400–350 B.C.E. (see p. 10).

Composition of the text

For the past century the unity of the text has been debated. Some scholars maintained that it was a work composed of two parts by two different authors. Others modified this position or emphasized its unity. Recent scholars suggest that the book has a literary unity. They refer to thematic connections, such as "the day of the Lord" (1:15; 2:1; 3:4; 4:14) and parallel expressions (2:27 and 4:17). Commentators debate whether the literary unity is the work of one author or of a few authors who edited the chapters for its present canonical shape.

Outline of the book

There are differences in the numbering of the chapters and verses in the second part of the Book of Joel. This commentary is based on the New American Bible, which uses the Hebrew text; other Bibles and commentaries may use the Greek text. The chart compares the two versions:

Hebrew Text	Greek Text
3:1-5	2:28-32
4:1-8	3:1-8
4:9-16	3:9-16
4:17-21	3:17-21

In this commentary the numbering of the Greek text is given in brackets:

PART ONE:	The Plague of Locusts and the Community (1:1–2:17)
1:1-4	Plague of Locusts
1:5-20	Call to Lamentation
2:1-11	Great Alarm
2:12-17	Call to Repentance
PART TWO:	The Response of the Lord to Israel and the Nations (2:18–4:21 [2:18–3:21])
2:18-27	Compassion for the Community
3:1-5 [2:28-32]	Blessings for the Community
4:1-17 [3:1-17]	Judgment on the Nations
4:18-21 [3:18-21]	Presence of God in Jerusalem

The Book of Joel

Text and Commentary

1 **The Land Invaded.** ¹The word of the LORD which came to Joel, the son of Pethuel.

²Hear this, you elders!
Pay attention, all you who dwell in the land!
Has the like of this happened in your days,
or in the days of your fathers?
³Tell it to your children,
and your children to their children,
and their children to the next generation.

PART ONE: THE PLAGUE OF LOCUSTS AND THE COMMUNITY

Joel 1:1–2:17

Situations of catastrophe prompted special liturgies to respond to a particular disaster within the community (see Judg 20:26; Jer 14:2, 7-9, 12). The Book of Joel is developed according to the structure of a communal lamentation. The components of the ritual were expanded for future generations until they attained the present canonical shape. This process broadened the possibilities for interpretation of the book.

Part One consists of two units (1:1-20 and 2:1-17). Both units indicate the structure of the first part of a lamentation liturgy: (a) a call to communal lamentation; (b) a cry and prayer of lamentation. The prophet calls together the Judeans of the temple-community to reflect on the catastrophe of the locust plague. He exhorts the entire community to mourn its devastated land, to repent, and to cry out to God for assistance. The plague is compared to the day of the Lord.

1:1-4 Plague of locusts. After the superscription of the book (v. 1), the setting is introduced. The prophet initiates a summons and exhortation to the community. The elders, leaders of the community in the postexilic era, are addressed (see Ezra 5:9; 6:7-8; compare Joel 1:2, 14; 2:17; 3:1). All the members of the community are called to consider whether the present disaster ever happened to their ancestors (v. 2). The rhetorical question is a common teaching tool, especially in the Writings of the Jewish canon, which preserved the accumulated wisdom of the people. Likewise, the prophet exhorts the community to hand down its experience of the plague to future generations (v. 3).

4What the cutter left,
  the locust swarm has eaten;
What the locust swarm left,
  the grasshopper has eaten;
And what the grasshopper left,
  the devourer has eaten.
5Wake up, you drunkards, and weep;
  wail, all you drinkers of wine,
Because the juice of the grape
  will be withheld from your mouths.
6For a people has invaded my land,
  mighty and without number;
His teeth are the teeth of a lion,
  and his molars those of a lioness.
7He has laid waste my vine,
and blighted my fig tree;
He has stripped it, sheared off its bark;
  its branches are made white.
8Lament like a virgin girt with sackcloth
  for the spouse of her youth.
9Abolished are offering and libation
  from the house of the LORD;
In mourning are the priests,
  the ministers of the LORD.

10The field is ravaged,
  the earth mourns,
Because the grain is ravaged,
  the must has failed,
  the oil languishes.

An initial description of the locusts appears as the climax of the setting (v. 4). "Cutter," "swarm," "grasshopper," and "devourer" may indicate stages of development in the life-cycle of locusts. How they destroy crops is suggested by the triple reference to the fact that *what (is) left* at each stage is *eaten* by the next stage. The damage that the locusts cause is attested to in biblical and extrabiblical literature. The last recorded plague in Jerusalem is reported to have been in A.D. 1915.

1:5-20 Call to lamentation. Verses 5-14 address members of the community for whom the results of the plague are overwhelming. Exhortations to particular actions refer to ritual activities associated with the liturgy of lamentation. Four groups of people are highlighted:

1) Imbibers of wine (vv. 5-7) are enjoined to "weep" and "wail" for the loss of sweet, new wine used to celebrate the autumn harvest festival (Exod 23:16). Like an invading army, the locusts have destroyed the vine.

2) The second group is not specified (vv. 8-10). It is probably a call to the entire community to "lament." The analogy of "a virgin girt with sackcloth for the spouse of her youth" (v. 8) refers to the mourning ritual of a woman after the first stage of relationship. The bridal price has been paid and public vows have been declared (see Deut 20:7; 22:23-24). The second stage, bringing the woman to her husband's home, has not occurred.

The image suggests deep, personal mourning. What type of loss could evoke such grief? Temple sacrifices have ceased because locusts ravaged the harvest (v. 9). The ritual ingredients of grain, wine, and oil are in short supply (v. 10). Significantly, the community's relationship with God symbolized in worship is severed.

3) Field workers and vinedressers (vv. 11-12) are told to "be appalled" and "wail." Their toil is futile. Their harvest, too, has failed. The yield is

¹¹Be appalled, you' husbandmen!
  wail, you vinedressers!
Over the wheat and the barley,
  because the harvest of the field has
    perished.
¹²The vine has dried up,
  the fig tree is withered;
The pomegranate, the date palm also,
    and the apple,
  all the trees of the field are dried up;
Yes, joy has withered away
  from among mankind.

Call to Penance

¹³Gird yourselves and weep, O priests!
  wail, O ministers of the altar!
Come, spend the night in sackcloth,
  O ministers of my God!
The house of your God is deprived
  of offering and libation.
¹⁴Proclaim a fast,
  call an assembly;
Gather the elders,
  all who dwell in the land,
Into the house of the LORD, your God,

"dried up" and "withered." In particular, the land often interpreted as a sign of God's blessing for Israel has now become a curse. Like the produce, "joy has withered away" in the community.

4) Priests (vv. 13-14) are exhorted to "gird [themselves] . . . weep . . . wail." The instruction repeats the directives given to the other groups, with additional stipulations: (a) They are to spend day and *night* in sackcloth, a custom invoked only in extreme situations (see 2 Sam 12:16; 1 Kgs 21:27). (b) As "ministers of the altar," their ritual activity is located in the "house of your God," the temple, where sacrifice is no longer held (v. 13; compare v. 9). (c) Their office authorizes them to announce a fast, to summon and assemble the leaders and the entire community. The formal liturgy of lamentation is convened in the "house of the Lord, your God" (v. 14).

Verses 2 and 14 comprise an inclusion mentioning the "elders" and "all who dwell in the land." Its function is to draw attention to a literary unit by separating particular verses from the text. Here verses 2-14 describe the members of the community gathered for lamentation.

A cry and a prayer of lamentation follow (vv. 15-20). An exclamation of sorrow is attached to the day of the Lord, which is identified as "near" and as a day of "ruin from the Almighty" (v. 15). The statement was alarming to the community for two reasons. First, according to prophetic oracles, the day of the Lord meant God's judgment against the enemies of Israel, "the nations" (see Isa 13:6; Ezek 30:2-3; Jer 46:10). Later the oracles included the judgment of Israel for disobeying God (see Amos 5:18-20; Lam 2:22; Ezek 34:12). After the destruction of Jerusalem (586 B.C.E.), the threatening oracles appeared to be fulfilled. Second, according to the postexilic community, the day of the Lord was considered a future event limited to the nations.

In addition, the prophet invites the community to consider its present situation with a rhetorical question regarding the scanty food supply and the absence of sacrifices (v. 16; compare v. 2). Both persons and animals starve

and cry to the LORD!

¹⁵Alas, the day!
for near is the day of the LORD,
and it comes as ruin from the Almighty.
¹⁶From before our very eyes
has not the food been cut off;
And from the house of our God,
joy and gladness?
¹⁷The seed lies shriveled under its clods;
the stores are destroyed,
The barns are broken down,
for the grain has failed.
¹⁸How the beasts groan!
The herds of cattle are bewildered!
Because they have no pasturage,
even the flocks of sheep have perished.
¹⁹To you, O LORD, I cry!
for fire has devoured the pastures of
the plain,
and flame has enkindled all the trees
of the field.
²⁰Even the beasts of the field

cry out to you;
For the streams of water are dried up,
and fire has devoured the pastures of
the plain.

The Day of the Lord

2 ¹Blow the trumpet in Zion,
sound the alarm on my holy mountain!
Let all who dwell in the land tremble,
for the day of the LORD is coming;
²Yes, it is near, a day of darkness and of
gloom,
a day of clouds and somberness!
Like dawn spreading over the mountains,
a people numerous and mighty!
Their like has not been from of old,
nor will it be after them,
even to the years of distant generations.
³Before them a fire devours,
and after them a flame enkindles;
Like the garden of Eden is the land before them,

because the locusts have devoured their sustenance (vv. 17-18). The joy especially characteristic of the community at harvest festivals and worship is banished (v. 16; compare v. 12). The clear parallelism between the day of the Lord and the devastation of the plague suggests that the prophet may be interpreting the plague as a foreshadowing of the day of the Lord for the community.

A prayer (vv. 19-20) concludes the first unit of Part One. It is structured according to many psalms of lamentation: an invocation to God and a statement of complaint (vv. 19b-20; compare Pss 12:1-3; 74:1). "Fire has devoured" is a repeated metaphor to describe the locusts as the source of the complaint (vv. 19a; 20b).

2:1-11 Great alarm. This section and 2:12-17 constitute the second unit of Part One. The relationship of 1:2-20 and 2:1-17 is problematic. A few commentators state that 2:1-17 is a doublet. Some prefer to draw literary and theological parallels. Others emphasize the differences between the two sections. Canonical critics suggest that the parallels and redaction are clues as to how later communities of believers interpreted the book.

The section compared with 1:2-14 indicates parallels and differences. Some elements are nearly identical. Catastrophe is the focus. While 1:2-14 described

and after them a desert waste;
from them there is no escape.
⁴Their appearance is that of horses;
like steeds they run.
⁵As with the rumble of chariots
they leap on the mountaintops;
As with the crackling of a fiery flame
devouring stubble;
Like a mighty people
arrayed for battle.
⁶Before them peoples are in torment,
every face blanches.
⁷Like warriors they run,
like soldiers they scale the wall;
They advance, each in his own lane,
without swerving from their paths.
⁸No one crowds another,
each advances in his own track;

Though they fall into the ditches,
they are not checked.
⁹They assault the city,
they run upon the wall,
they climb into the houses;
In at the windows
they come like thieves.
¹⁰Before them the earth trembles,
the heavens shake;
The sun and the moon are darkened,
and the stars withhold their brightness.
¹¹The LORD raises his voice
at the head of his army;
For immense indeed is his camp,
yes, mighty, and it does his bidding.
For great is the day of the LORD,

the *results* of the locust invasion, 2:1-11 describes the *agents* of the catastrophe. The images that alluded to the relationship of the plague to the day of the Lord (1:15-20) are repeated. The proclamation is addressed to members of the temple-community. The time-sequence, however, is different. The locust plague is an event of the *past*; the day of the Lord is *imminent.* A second difference is the addition of metaphors to indicate other characteristics of the event.

The new section indicates a parallel setting (2:1-3; compare 1:2-4). Approaching danger is announced to "all who dwell in the land" with the blast of the "trumpet" (v. 1; compare 1:2, 14). The *shofar,* or ram's horn, sounded an alarm for battle as well as a call for the community to assemble in worship. The day of the Lord is the source of anxiety. The event is also heralded by cosmic signs (compare Zeph 1:14-15) and an unprecedented enemy (v. 2; see 1:6). Like "devouring fire" (see 1:4, 19), the oppressor transforms the "garden of Eden" into a "desert waste" (v. 3; compare 1:20).

A series of metaphors developed according to strength, skill, and terror identifies the day of the Lord in the context of battle (vv. 4-9). The details may resemble a description of the "holy war." Some scholars consider the event as an early stage of the day of the Lord. The metaphors are: running and leaping horses, dragging chariots behind them (vv. 4-5a); a crackling, devouring flame (v. 5b; compare 1:19; 2:3); a mighty people arrayed for battle (v. 5b); warriors and soldiers running and scaling the wall with disciplined routine, assaulting the city and climbing into the houses (vv. 7-9). Two groups are affected. Anguish colors the victims' faces (v. 6; compare Isa 13:8). The cosmic forces (earth, heavens, sun, moon, stars) quake and darken (v. 10).

and exceedingly terrible; who can bear it?
¹²Yet even now, says the LORD,
return to me with your whole heart,
with fasting, and weeping, and mourning;
¹³Rend your hearts, not your garments,
and return to the LORD, your God.
For gracious and merciful is he,

slow to anger, rich in kindness,
and relenting in punishment.
¹⁴Perhaps he will again relent
and leave behind him a blessing,
Offerings and libations
for the LORD, your God.
¹⁵Blow the trumpet in Zion!
proclaim a fast,
call an assembly;

The image of the holy war continues with the appearance of the Lord as the leader of the army (v. 11a). The section concludes with an inclusion, the day of the Lord (vv. 1a and 11b). The short comment "who can bear it?" appears to be a postscript, another example of the rhetorical question noted above (1:2b, 16b).

2:12-17 Call to repentance. This section is constructed to provide connections with the first part of the unit (2:1-11). It also indicates structural and thematic parallels and differences when compared with 1:5-20. The verses suggest an immediate response to the day of the Lord (2:1-11), just as the plague of locusts in the first unit demanded a response. Both events are followed by an exhortation to communal lamentation.

Verses 12 and 13 indicate an unusual circumstance to alter the awesome day of the Lord. The revelation reverses the poignant more-than-rhetorical-question of section one, to which it is structurally connected (v. 11b). God's proclamation, "Yet even now, says the Lord" (v. 12a), presents a possibility other than imminent gloom and destruction (2:1-11). It offers hope to the community trembling from the locust invasion and fearfully awaiting the worse event.

What is suggested? The invitation is to "return to me with your whole heart, with fasting, and weeping, and mourning" (v. 12b; see Amos 4:6-11; Hos 3:5; 14:2). The language indicates a turning toward God with one's whole being, the complete reorientation of thoughts and decisions toward God. Participation in a communal liturgy of lamentation (fasting, weeping, mourning) is encouraged. The ritual will symbolize the process of the community's commitment to God.

Verse 13b is a reaffirmation of the earlier relationship of God and the community revealed in the covenant at Mount Sinai (compare Exod 34:6-7). God is gracious, merciful, kind, relenting in punishment. The members of the present community are dependent upon a new manifestation of God's mercy. God *may* relent. The community is challenged to "return." Only then will there be the restored blessing of "offerings and libations," symbols of the relationship of God and the community (v. 14; compare 1:9, 12, 16).

23

¹⁶Gather the people,
   notify the congregation;
Assemble the elders,
   gather the children
   and the infants at the breast;
Let the bridegroom quit his room,
   and the bride her chamber.
¹⁷Between the porch and the altar
   let the priests, the ministers of the
   Lord, weep,

And say, "Spare, O Lord, your people,
   and make not your heritage a reproach,
   with the nations ruling over them!
Why should they say among the
   peoples,
   'Where is their God?' "

Blessings for God's People. ¹⁸Then the Lord was stirred to concern for his land

The new possibility for the community gives a sense of urgency to the ritual of lamentation (vv. 15-17). The ritual actions to initiate the liturgy repeat earlier directions (v. 15; 1:14; 2:1). Additional components comprise this summons:

a) Children, infants, bride and bridegroom are included in the assembly. The gravity of the situation and the witness of "all who dwell in the land" preclude any exceptions for privileges ordinarily given to a young couple (v. 16; compare Deut 24:5).

b) The location for the officials of the service is indicated: "between the porch and the altar" (v. 17a). It is the traditional place for leading the community in lamentation. The distance may refer to the lack of sacrifices due to the locust invasion as well as the symbolic interpretation of strained relationships between the community and God (compare Ezek 8:16).

The prayer of lamentation (v. 17b) that concludes the section differs from the one recorded in 1:19-20. The priests implore God to spare the community, "your people," and to prevent "your heritage" from becoming "a reproach with the nations ruling over them." The plea is a traditional one (Pss 42:4; 79:10; 115:2). Here the collective experience of Israel mirrors the current situation. A rhetorical question is attributed to the nations. It ironically emphasizes their interpretation of the community's plight: "Where is their God?"

PART TWO: THE RESPONSE OF THE LORD TO ISRAEL AND THE NATIONS

Joel 2:18–4:21 [2:18–3:21]

Part One and Part Two constitute identical literary and topical structures. Each part is constructed with two units. Each unit contains two sections. Each part refers to a particular stage of the communal lamentation liturgy. In addition, the ordering of Part One and Part Two follows a chronology of events (locust invasion and imminent day of the Lord); the order of a

and took pity on his people. ¹⁹The LORD answered and said to his people:

See, I will send you
grain, and wine, and oil,
and you shall be filled with them;
No more will I make you
a reproach among the nations.

²⁰No, the northerner I will remove far from you,
and drive him out into a land arid and waste,
With his van toward the eastern sea,
and his rear toward the western sea;
And his foulness shall go up,
and his stench shall go up.

lamentation service (stage one and stage two); and a development of prophetic revelation.

Part Two consists of two units: 2:18–3:5 [2:18-32] and 4:1-21 [3:1-21]. Both units indicate the structure of the second part of a communal service: a series of oracles containing divine assurance. The proclamations respond to the plea of the community suffering the results of the locusts and fearing the approaching day of the Lord. They promise a *future* of restoration and *new* blessings to reverse the characteristics of the day of the Lord.

In addition to the consistencies in Part One and Part Two, some commentators have identified a new literary genre in Joel 3:1–4:21 [2:28–3:21], namely, proto-apocalyptic (see p. 15). Characteristics of this genre which describe preliminaries to the day of the Lord include: outpouring of the spirit, cosmic signs, judgment against the nations, and blessings for the community.

2:18-27 Compassion for the community. This section describes a restoration of the community's situation by God. Verse 18 provides the transition from Part One to Part Two. God's concerns are the land and the people. The phrase "stirred to concern" is better translated "became jealous" (Revised Standard Version). It indicates the passionate zeal of God *for* the community (see Ezek 39:25; Zech 1:14; 8:2). God responds to the plight of the community with compassion. Subsequent activity is detailed in the assurances about restored life and freedom from enemies. They are presented in three consecutive oracles:

1) Assurances are introduced (vv. 19-20). God will send supplies needed for sustenance and sacrifice: "grain," "wine," "oil" (v. 19a; compare 1:7, 9-11, 13b, 16-17; 2:14). The community will no longer be "a reproach among the nations" (v. 19b; compare 2:17). Verse 20 describes the "northerner," which may refer to the locusts as well as their symbolic counterpart, the army of invaders (see 2:1-11). Hostile forces often approached from the north (see Jer 1:14, 15; 4:6; Ezek 38:6; 39:2). Here the enemy is destroyed by expulsion to an "arid and waste" land and by drowning in the sea.

2) "Fear not" oracles are addressed to the land and the animals connected with the community (vv. 21-22). Both are assured of verdant and fruitful life (compare 1:10-12).

²¹Fear not, O land!
exult and rejoice!
for the Lord has done great things.
²²Fear not, beasts of the field!
for the pastures of the plain are green;
The tree bears its fruit,
the fig tree and the vine give their
yield.
²³And do you, O children of Zion, exult
and rejoice in the Lord, your God!
He has given you the teacher of justice:
he has made the rain come down for
you,
the early and the late rain as before.
²⁴The threshing floors shall be full of grain
and the vats shall overflow with wine
and oil.
²⁵And I will repay you for the years
which the locust has eaten,
The grasshopper, the devourer, and the
cutter,
my great army which I sent among
you.
²⁶You shall eat and be filled,
and shall praise the name of the Lord,
your God,
Because he has dealt wondrously with
you;
my people shall nevermore be put to
shame.
²⁷And you shall know that I am in the
midst of Israel;
I am the Lord, your God, and there is
no other;
my people shall nevermore be put to
shame.

3 ¹Then afterward I will pour out
my spirit upon all mankind.

3) Instruction and promises are announced to the temple-community, "children of Zion" (vv. 23-27; Lam 4:2; Ps 149:2). The group is invited to "rejoice in the Lord, your God!" (v. 23a). The second part of the verse is obscure. The New American Bible has God giving the community a "teacher of justice: he has made the rain come down for you." The Revised Standard Version has God as the giver of "the early rain for your vindication." Both translations point to God who restores a favorable condition for harvest by providing rain at the proper seasons.

This favorable situation, in turn, provides supplies for temple sacrifice. "Justice" and "vindication" suggest the ritual act of worship, which represents the covenant relationship of God and the community. The daily sacrifices at the temple had ceased because of the locust invasion.

The next three verses support the interpretation. God will provide grain, wine, and oil in great abundance as restitution for the destruction of the locusts (vv. 24-25; see 1:4; 2:5-9). Needs for sustenance and for worshiping God will be satisfied (v. 26; compare Ps 126:3).

A recognition formula concludes the section (v. 27). It indicates a new understanding of God for the community. God will be in their midst. No other god is comparable to the God of Israel. The community will "nevermore be put to shame" (compare Exod 20:2-3). The reference may be to the disgrace of the Exile (v. 26). The revelation of the new relationship is a climax to the section as well as a response to the taunt of the nations: "Where is their God?" (2:17).

Your sons and daughters shall prophesy,
your old men shall dream dreams,
your young men shall see visions;
²Even upon the servants and the handmaids,

in those days, I will pour out my
spirit.

³And I will work wonders in the heavens
and on the earth,
blood, fire, and columns of smoke;

3:1-5 [2:28-32] Blessings for the community. These verses are connected thematically to 2:18-27. Both describe the characteristics of future restoration in successive stages. "Then afterward" (3:1) provides the transition to a new time-sequence. It presupposes that the conditions of restoration that God promised (2:18-27) have been fulfilled. It points to an uncertain time in the future when God's new blessings (3:1-5 [2:28-32]) will be realized in the community. The section is structured according to three blessings. Each is outlined in a three-line stanza:

1) Participation in God's spirit (vv. 1-2 [2:28-29]). "All mankind" identifies the members of the temple-community (2:19, 27; compare 4:2, 17, 19-21). The Revised Standard Version translates the Hebrew as "flesh" to emphasize the contrast between human weakness (see Isa 40:6; Ps 56:5) and God's vital power, which will transform their lives. The promise is radical, for Jewish tradition had limited God's spirit to persons with official status: a judge, like Gideon (Judg 6:34); a king, like Saul (1 Sam 16:14); a prophet, like Ezekiel (Ezek 2:2). Although Moses desired a spirit-filled community (Num 11:29), God's spirit had been limited to the seventy elders (Num 11:17, 25).

In these verses God's spirit will empower each member of the community to "prophesy." The activity is further clarified with corresponding terms: "dream dreams" and "see visions." The "prophets" are identified as "your sons and daughters," "your old men," and "your young men" (v. 1b). What is unusual is the mention of "servants" and "handmaids" (v. 2). Although their rights were protected according to the law for the sabbath rest (Exod 20:10) and festivals (Deut 12:12, 18; 16:11, 14), they were not considered members of the community. Participation in God's spirit implies *equal* status for each person in the community.

The author of Luke-Acts quotes and interprets Joel 3:1-5a [2:28-32a] in the account of Peter's discourse at Pentecost (Acts 2:17-21). The risen Lord received the Spirit from God, "then poured this Spirit out on us" (Acts 2:33). Greek and Jew alike have access to the Spirit if they believe in Jesus and are baptized (Acts 2:38).

2) Cosmic signs (vv. 3-4 [2:30-31]). The activity of God on behalf of the Israelites during the Exodus (1250 B.C.E.) included wonders with blood (Exod 24:4-8), fire and smoke (Exod 13:21-22; 19:18). These elements (v. 3) and the eclipse of the sun (v. 4a; compare Rev 6:12) also indicate traditional im-

⁴The sun will be turned to darkness,
  and the moon to blood,
At the coming of the day of the LORD,
  the great and terrible day.
⁵Then everyone shall be rescued
  who calls on the name of the LORD;
For on Mount Zion there shall be a remnant,

as the LORD has said,
And in Jerusalem survivors
  whom the LORD shall call.

Judgment upon the Nations

4 ¹Yes, in those days, and at that time,
  when I would restore the fortunes
  of Judah and Jerusalem,

agery associated with the terrible day of the Lord (see p. 22). The identification of cosmic signs as blessings becomes clear when the verses are considered
as portents of the day of the Lord, when something *unexpected* will occur
(v. 5).

3) Deliverance (v. 5 [2:32]). Rescue is assured for each person who "calls
on the name of the Lord" (v. 5a). The directive includes recognition of God
(Exod 33:19) and worship (Isa 12:4; Ps 105:1; compare Zech 13:9) before
the nations. Those designated as "the rescued" are further identified in verse
5bc as a "remnant" and "survivors." Their home is located on "Mount Zion"
and in "Jerusalem." The descriptions indicate the temple-community of Judah
preeminently. Some commentators suggest that the descriptions may include
the Jews of the Diaspora (see Isa 27:12-13; 57:19), that is, Jews living outside
Israel.

Paul introduces verse 5a in Rom 10:12-13 by interpreting its significance
universally: "Here there is no difference between Jew and Greek; all have
the same Lord, rich in mercy toward all who call upon him" (Rom 10:12).
The outpouring of the Spirit at Pentecost is interpreted similarly: "It was
to you and your children that the promise was made, and to all those still
far off whom the Lord our God calls" (Acts 2:39).

Recognition of earlier prophetic tradition is acknowledged in the clause
"as the Lord has said" (v. 5b). The use of "remnant" terminology interprets
Obad 17a: "But on Mount Zion there shall be a portion saved; the mountain
shall be holy." The prophet also specified the source of life for the "remnant" by drawing on Ezek 39:29: "No longer will I hide my face from them,
for I have poured out my spirit on the house of Israel, says the Lord God."

"Survivors whom the Lord shall call" (v. 5c) is a recognition of the mutual relationship between the Lord and the community that "calls upon the
name of the Lord" (v. 5a). In 3:1-5 [2:28-32] there is the recognition that
God's community will continue. A community whose home is in Jerusalem
will be given God's spirit to function as prophets.

4:1-17 [3:1-17] Judgment on the nations. This section continues the
theme of Part Two: Response of the Lord to Israel and the Nations. The circumstances of the community's suffering at the hands of the nations are

²I will assemble all the nations
and bring them down to the Valley of Jehoshaphat,
And I will enter into judgment with them there
on behalf of my people and my inheritance, Israel;
Because they have scattered them among the nations,
and divided my land.
³Over my people they have cast lots;
they gave a boy for a harlot,
and sold a girl for the wine they drank.
⁴Moreover, what are you to me, Tyre and Sidon, and all the regions of Philistia? Would you take vengeance upon me by some action? But if you do take action against me, swiftly, speedily, I will return your deed upon your own head. ⁵You took my silver and my gold, and brought my precious treasures into your temples! ⁶You sold the people of Judah and Jerusalem to the Greeks, removing them far

reviewed. They prescribe God's action and judgment against Israel's enemies consistent with traditional imagery associated with the day of the Lord. Two later additions occur in the text (vv. 4-8, 18-21).

The introduction for the section (vv. 1-3 [3:1-3] states the reasons for God's judgment. Verse 1 is a transition linking the theme of restoration for the community (2:17–3:5 [2:17-32]) with the consequences of its enemies (3:2-17 [2:32–3:17]). In verse 1 the community is designated initially as "Judah" and "Jerusalem"; in verses 2 and 3, however, it is described in relation to God: "*my* people" (see 2:17, 27; 4:3); "*my* inheritance" (see 2:17); "*my* land."

God will assemble all the nations for judgment (v. 2a). The "Valley of Jehoshaphat" is probably cited more for its connection to the Hebrew phrase ("Yahweh judges") than for its location as a specific geographical area. In early Christian tradition the historian Eusebius (*Onamastikon*) identified the place as the Kidron Valley. In verse 14b the place is referred to as the "valley of decision."

The nations are indicted for three actions toward the community which occurred during earlier Jewish history and continued through the time of Joel (vv. 2b-3):

1) "Scattered among the nations" refers to the deportations led by Assyria and Babylon from the eighth century through the sixth century. The exilic experience of Judah and Jerusalem, in particular, is recalled here.

2) "And divided my land" describes the immediate accessibility to the land for the conquerors who settled there (see Lam 5:2).

3) "Over my people they have cast lots" indicates how little the victors valued the lives of the deportees (see Obad 11; Nah 3:10). Children, in particular, are described as the victims of their pleasures.

The prose addition (vv. 4-8 [3:4-8]) elaborates the guilt of the nations resulting from their treatment of Israel (vv. 1-3). It suggests a courtroom nar-

from their own country! ⁷See, I will rouse them from the place into which you have sold them, and I will return your deed upon your own head. ⁸I will sell your sons and your daughters to the people of Judah, who shall sell them to the Sabeans, a nation far off. Indeed, the LORD has spoken.

⁹Declare this among the nations:
proclaim a war,
rouse the warriors to arms!
Let all the soldiers
report and march!
¹⁰Beat your plowshares into swords,
and your pruning hooks into spears;
let the weak man say, "I am a warrior!"

¹¹Hasten and come, all you neighboring peoples,
assemble there!

[Bring down, O Lord, your warriors!]
¹²Let the nations bestir themselves and come up
to the Valley of Jehoshaphat;
For there will I sit in judgment
upon all the neighboring nations.

¹³Apply the sickle,
for the harvest is ripe;
Come and tread,
for the wine press is full;
The vats overflow,
for great is their malice.

¹⁴Crowd upon crowd
in the valley of decision;
For near is the day of the LORD
in the valley of decision.

¹⁵Sun and moon are darkened,
and the stars withhold their brightness.

rative, with God functioning as accuser, judge, and vindicator of the community. To open the trial, God poses a rhetorical question about taking vengeance and promises swift retribution. Tyre, Sidon, and the regions of Philistia (the addressees) refer to territories of traditional animosity toward Israel. Next, God condemns specific actions against the community: plundering the temple, selling persons as slaves to the Greeks, sending them into exile (vv. 5-6). Finally, God promises exact retaliation for their deeds. For engaging in slave trade (see Amos 1:6-10; Ezek 27:13), they will be sold as slaves to the community. As dealers, the community will exile its former enemies by bartering with the Sabeans. The scene concludes with a statement of divine authority: "Indeed the Lord has spoken" (vv. 7-8).

The third division in the section (vv. 9-16 [3:9-16]) continues the poetic and thematic structure of the introduction (vv. 1-3). The Valley of Jehoshaphat is the site for judgment (v. 12) and for battle (v. 14). Unknown addressees are exhorted to announce war, rouse the soldiers, and assemble the peoples roundabout (vv. 9-11). The dire situation implies additional soldiers. The untrained warriors—farmers and field workers—are urged to respond. The directive is an ironic one that intentionally *reverses* the call to peace declared in earlier prophetic traditions (v. 10; see Isa 2:4; Mic 4:3).

Instructions associated with harvest, "apply the sickle," "come and tread" (v. 13), now identify the ferocious battle waged against the enemies of the community. The event is closely aligned to the imminent day of the Lord (v. 14). Additional cosmic imagery heralds the day (vv. 15-16). The Lord

¹⁶The LORD roars from Zion,
  and from Jerusalem raises his voice;
The heavens and the earth quake,
  but the LORD is a refuge to his people,
  a stronghold to the men of Israel.

Salvation for God's Elect

¹⁷Then shall you know that I, the LORD,
  am your God,
  dwelling on Zion, my holy mountain;
Jerusalem shall be holy,
  and strangers shall pass through her
  no more.
¹⁸And then, on that day,
  the mountains shall drip new wine,
  and the hills shall flow with milk;

And the channels of Judah
  shall flow with water:
A fountain shall issue from the house of
  the LORD,
  to water the Valley of Shittim.
¹⁹Egypt shall be a waste,
  and Edom a desert waste,
Because of violence done to the people
  of Judah,
  because they shed innocent blood in
  their land.
²⁰But Judah shall abide forever,
  and Jerusalem for all generations.
²¹I will avenge their blood,
  and not leave it unpunished.
The LORD dwells in Zion.

dwelling in Zion "roars" and "raises his voice" (v. 16a; compare 2:11a). The action does not indicate anger but *protection* for the community, for whom the Lord is a "refuge" and "stronghold" (v. 16b; see Pss 31:3-5; 61:4).

The climax to the section is a summary declaration of the oracles of assurance and blessing. The ultimate security for the community is knowing that the Lord is "your God," dwelling among them, providing the source of holiness and protection from all enemies (v. 17 [3:17]).

4:18-21 [3:18-21] Presence of God in Jerusalem. This poetic insertion may be regarded as an appendix to the Book of Joel. It amplifies the major theme of restoration by a series of promises to be fulfilled "on that day":

a) abundant sustenance for the community: wine, milk, water (v. 18; see Amos 9:13b; Ezek 47:1-12);

b) the destruction of Egypt and Edom, enduring political enemies (v. 19; see 1 Kgs 14:25; Obad 8-14);

c) everlasting security for Judah and Jerusalem (v. 20; see 3:5; 4:16);

d) retribution for enemies and the presence of the Lord in Zion (v. 21).

Conclusion

A literary analysis of the Book of Joel suggests the structure of a communal liturgy of lamentation. The format, however, has been expanded and developed by editorial activity. While many commentators recognize the development of the book, there is no consensus about the number of persons involved in this process. Some commentators see no connection between the literary development of the book and its religious meaning. They interpret the book according to a few general perspectives:

a) The book presents a restricted, nationalistic point of view. God's promises of restoration are limited to the Zion community in fulfillment of earlier prophetic traditions. Often Joel is compared unfavorably with the breadth of Isaiah and Micah, who include the participation of the nations in the community of Jerusalem (see Isa 2:2-4; Mic 4:1-3).

b) The importance of the book is virtually dependent on the figure of Jesus. He is the fulfillment of the prophecies by dying for the "nations" and giving the Spirit to all who believed in him.

c) Jews and Christians await a future event that will surpass the expectations of restoration that Joel proclaimed (see Rev 21).

Canonical critics offer a different perspective on the relationship of the literary development of Joel and its religious meaning. *How* the Book of Joel emerged as a canonical text provides clues to its religious significance in future communities.

Sources available for the editorial process included the original prophecy of Joel, presenting the devastation of the locust plague, and images and terms describing the day of the Lord taken from earlier prophetic traditions. In arranging and adding to the sources, the editor(s) shaped the text to provide a message for future communities. References to the new addressees are indicated initially in the introduction to the first part of the book (1:3). The entire second part of the book (2:18–4:21 [2:18–3:21]), with its proclamations about future possibilities, is also fashioned to include them.

The editorial process provided a continuity of religious experience and hope for the original community and for future communities. It shaped the book to declare that God's compassion toward the temple-community of Judah because of their repentance would be possible for any community. Correspondingly, the blessings of restoration would be possible for future communities as well. For both types of community, original and future, neither final judgment nor blessings had definitively occurred.

The perspective of canonical critics appears preferable to the interpretation of other commentators because it assumes that a text can be valuable for its own contribution. Consequently, the methodology does not depend on prophecy-fulfillment in the New Testament or on comparison with other prophetic traditions in the Old Testament to validate the importance of the Book of Joel. Canonical criticism provides a necessary focus on the placement of Joel within the Minor Prophets. It also widens the interpretation of Joel through a different methodology that includes implications for future communities.

The Book of Obadiah

Introduction

Authorship

What is known about the author of this book is limited to verse 1a, which names and identifies him: "The vision of Obadiah. [Thus says the Lord God:] Of Edom we have heard a message from the Lord." "Vision" is a technical term for prophecy (see Nah 1:1; Mic 1:1), whose contents are described in verses 2-4. "We have heard a message . . .," however, emphasizes that auditory perception is the source for prophetic inspiration. "[Thus says the Lord God:]" and the repetition of the divine name also indicate traditional prophetic formulas. The name Obadiah means "servant of Yahweh." It occurs twelve times in the Hebrew Scriptures. In the Book of Obadiah the name may be used more for its symbolic sense.

Other biographical detail is inferred from the text. Many scholars suggest that Obadiah was a cult prophet attached to the Jerusalem temple before its destruction (586 B.C.E.). The structure of the prophecies reflects a liturgical service in which the sovereignty of God is affirmed through oracles against the nations. Obadiah's connection with the temple in Jerusalem is strengthened by references to God's kingdom and Mount Zion (vv. 17, 21). Other scholars suggest that an unknown prophet utilized a liturgical structure for the deliverance of oracles.

Dating of the text

The superscription of the book indicates no chronological setting for Obadiah. The position of the book in the canons is not decisive for establishing a date. The Jewish canon lists Obadiah after Amos (preexilic), while the Alexandrian canon locates Obadiah after Joel (postexilic).

While most scholars agree that the oracles against Edom were proclaimed after 586 B.C.E., the dating of the final text is disputed. The present discussion involves a consideration of the relationship between Israel and Edom, oral and written traditions, and the process of editorial activity.

According to Jewish tradition, the relationship between Israel and Edom was one of continuous conflict. It is attributed to the fraternal conflict of two brothers, Jacob and Esau (see Gen 25:19-34; 26:34-35; 27:1-44; 32:4;

33:1-17). The hostility developed for several centuries as the descendants of Jacob (Israelites) and Esau (Edomites) refused one another rights of territorial passage (see Num 20:14-21) and freedom (see 2 Sam 8:13-14; 1 Kgs 11:15-18).

Edom revolted against Judah about 844 B.C.E. The animosity between them continued, however, for nearly 250 additional years, culminating in Edom's alliance with Babylon against Judah (see p. 8). Although the extent of Edomite activity against Judah during this period is unclear, the witness of the anti-Edom oracles (see below) indict Edom for treachery and betrayal. There is even a claim that the Edomites burned the temple (see 1 Esdras 4:45). They probably conspired with the Babylonian empire and settled in Judean territory.

A recent archeological investigation supports this position. It uncovered an inscription contemporary with the last days of Jerusalem. A troop commander in Arad sent for additional soldiers to fortify a position against an imminent Edomite attack: "Behold I have sent to warn you: are not the men with Elisha, lest Edom come thither."

Edom, unlike Judah, was independent but not untroubled for over a hundred years after the fall of Jerusalem. Tribes from Arabia frequently raided the land (see Mal 1:2-4). After 450 B.C.E. the name Edom disappeared from historical records. During the reign of Herod the Great (37–4 B.C.E.), however, the territory designated Edom was named Idumea. *Mekiltha*, a Jewish text of the early Christian period, identified Edom as a code name for oppression.

Commentators suggest that the enmity between Israel and Edom was preserved in oral traditions that were later recorded as anti-Edom oracles. While some fragments are located in the Jacob cycle (see Gen 25:23; 27:39-40), the most extensive witness is located outside the Torah (see Isa 21:11-12; 34:5-7; 63:1-6; Jer 49:7-22; Lam 4:21-22; Ezek 25:12-14; 35:1-5; Amos 1:11-12; Mal 1:3-5; Ps 137:7-9). In these passages Edom is condemned for less dramatic but more continuous harassment than burning the temple.

Part of the complexity involved in dating the Book of Obadiah is the relationship of the anti-Edom oracles (vv. 1-14, 15b) to Jer 49:7-22. Some commentators state that Obadiah represented the prior tradition, while others indicate that Jeremiah was the first witness to the tradition. A third group traces both Obadian and Jeremian oracles to a common earlier tradition. Both prophets incorporated the tradition and additional material after the fall of Jerusalem (586 B.C.E.).

Another question is the chronological relationship of the oracles in Obadiah. While condemnations of Edom predominate (vv. 1-14, 15b), there are oracles describing the day of the Lord (vv. 15a, 16-18) and the restoration of Israel (vv. 19-21). The difference of opinion about the approximate date of the oracles and subsequent editorial activity results in a final composition date from early postexilic (535 B.C.E.) to a century later (435 B.C.E.).

In this commentary Obadiah is identified first *chronologically* because of his proximity to the Edomite conspirators and redaction of earlier anti-Edom oracles. In addition, his position as a transitional figure between exilic and postexilic prophecy indicates a singular contribution among the other Minor Prophets. His contribution includes oracles against Edom after the destruction of Jerusalem as well as later oracles about the day of the Lord. These factors indicate that the date for the final edition of the text is a question of secondary importance.

Composition of the text

Although the Book of Obadiah is the shortest book of the Old Testament, discussion about the final dating of the text and related literary questions continues in the literature. There is no consensus about the priority of Jeremiah, Obadiah, or another common tradition for the anti-Edom oracles. In addition, the text has been analyzed according to two extreme positions: a literary unity or a collection of fragments. Presently, several commentators propose a moderate position. The book contains two sets of oracles and an appendix. Thematically, the unity of the oracles consists in Edom's condemnation and future situation in the day of the Lord. The appendix is related to Israel's restoration in that event.

Outline of the book

PART ONE:	Oracles against Edom (vv. 1-14, 15b)
vv. 1-9	Pride and Destruction of Edom
vv. 10-14	Treachery of Edom toward Judah
vv. 15b	Condemnation of Edom
PART TWO:	Oracles about the day of the Lord (vv. 15a, 16-21)
vv. 15a, 16	Judgment of the Nations
vv. 17-18	Return and Restoration of Israel
vv. 19-21	Appendix: Return and Restoration of Israel

The Book of Obadiah

Text and Commentary

Title and Theme
[1]The vision of Obadiah.
[Thus says the LORD God:]
Of Edom we have heard a message from the LORD,
and a herald has been sent among the nations:
"Up! let us go to war against him!"

PART ONE: ORACLES AGAINST EDOM

Obad 1-14, 15b

Part One is a collection of oracles that expand a common tradition of anti-Edom material. The closest parallel is Jer 49:7-22 (see p. 34). Commentators state that no more bitter diatribe exists against Edom in the whole of the Old Testament than what is recorded here.

Two perspectives are prominent about the interpretation of verses 2-9. The context of verses 1b and 7, in particular, is debated. Some suggest that the destruction of Edom has already occurred. The verses are an additional reflection on the event. Others indicate that the verses designate a future destruction. Attempts to establish the context are directly related to considerations of the dating and the composition of the text.

Proposals that seek to identify a specific historical event, that is, an Arabian conquest of Edom, appear to limit the possibilities for interpretation of the section. Although recent archeological discoveries are providing some limited support for this type of analysis, additional research and data are needed.

1-9 Pride and the destruction of Edom. Verse 1 is a prose introduction to the Book of Obadiah. It states his identity and function. It also links him to earlier prophetic tradition: "we have heard a message from the Lord" (v. 1a; see Jer 49:7).

Verse 1b relates the departure of a messenger to proclaim Edom's destruction among the nations: "Up! Let us go to war against him!" It is difficult to determine whether the statement refers to an *actual event,* that is, the approach of the Arabian enemy against Edom, or whether it is a *prophetic formula* of a war summons to the nations (Jer 49:14; Joel 4:9ff. [3:9ff.]; Mic 4:13).

Edom Shall Perish

²See, I make you small among the nations;
you are held in dire contempt.
³The pride of your heart has deceived you:
you who dwell in the clefts of the rock,
whose abode is in the heights,
Who say in your heart,
"Who will bring me down to earth?"

⁴Though you go as high as the eagle,
and your nest be set among the stars,
From there will I bring you down,

says the LORD.
⁵If thieves came to you, if robbers by night,
how could you be thus destroyed:
would they not steal merely till they had enough?
If vintagers came to you,
would they not leave some gleanings?
⁶How they search Esau,
seek out his hiding places!
⁷To the border they drive you—
all your allies;
They deceive you, they overpower you—
those at peace with you;

God announces the destruction of Edom (vv. 2-4; see Jer 49:14-16). The dispositions of the nation's heart are condemned. Pride effects Edom's contemptible position among the nations (v. 2). False security arises from dwelling "in the clefts of the rock" and "in the heights." The "rock" refers to the terrain as well as to the Edomite capital, Sela, a nearly impregnable city.

The arrogant challenge "Who will bring me down to earth?" will prove no obstacle to an enemy (v. 3). Even a position as an eagle with a nest among the stars will not thwart God's action: "I will bring you down" (v. 4; compare Amos 9:2; Isa 14:13-14).

God's power of destruction is compared to the strategy of prowlers invading homes in Edom (vv. 5-9). If "thieves," "robbers," or "vintagers" trespassed, they would leave something behind for the household (v. 5; see Jer 49:9; Lev 19:10; Deut 24:21). The destruction of Edom (Esau), however, will be without mercy. The event is described in a traditional cry of lament (vv. 6-7; see 2 Sam 1:19-27; Jer 38:22; Lam 1:1; 2:1; 4:1). It will be as thorough as the forfeit of Jacob's birthright to Esau (v. 6; see Gen 25:27-34). Those closest to the Edomites, allies and relatives, will participate in the devastation. "There is no understanding in him!" indicates the bewilderment and surprise that the event causes among the Edomites (v. 7).

Verse 7 is as difficult to interpret as verse 1. What are the implications of "allies" and "relatives"? Is it an ironic comment on the real but spurned relationships between Edom and Judah, which were completely severed in the fall of Jerusalem? Do the terms relate to the reversal of Judah's situation in the day of the Lord? (see Part Two). Do the bonds of relationship refer to those who supported Edom after the fall of Jerusalem but who later conquered Edom? The comment "There is no understanding in him" is appropriate for each interpretation.

Those who eat your bread
  lay snares beneath you:
  There is no understanding in him!
[8]Shall I not, says the LORD, on that day
  make the wise men disappear from
    Edom,
  and understanding from the mount of
    Esau?
[9]Your warriors, O Teman, shall be
    crushed,
  till all on Mount Esau are destroyed.

The Cause

[10]Because of violence to your brother
    Jacob,
  disgrace shall cover you
  and you shall be destroyed forever.
[11]On the day when you stood by,
  on the day when aliens carried off his
    possessions,

And strangers entered his gates
  and cast lots over Jerusalem,
  you too were one of them.
[12]Gaze not upon the day of your brother,
  the day of his disaster;
Exult not over the children of Judah
  on the day of their ruin;
Speak not haughtily
  on the day of distress!
[13]Enter not the gate of my people
  on the day of their calamity;
Gaze not, you at least, upon his mis-
    fortune
  on the day of his calamity;
Lay not hands upon his possessions
  on the day of his calamity!
[14]Stand not at the crossroads
  to slay his refugees;
Betray not his fugitives
  on the day of distress!

The divine formula "says the Lord" (v. 4) is repeated to form an inclusion expressing God's judgment against Edom (v. 8a). In a rhetorical question God states the disappearance of the "wise" and "understanding" from Edom (Esau). Their demise is related to verse 7, which also commented on "no understanding" (see Jer 49:7). The inhabitants of Edom and Arabia were traditionally considered wise persons (see 1 Kgs 5:10; 10:1-3; Job 1:1; 2:11; Prov 30:1; 31:1).

Warriors will be destroyed with the wise (v. 9). "Teman," an important city in Edom, refers to the whole territory. Another inclusive term is "Mount Esau" (vv. 8b, 9b).

10-14 Treachery of Edom toward Judah. The indictment against Edom is declared: "violence to your brother Jacob" (v. 10). Specifically, the condemnation is collaboration by passivity toward Babylon's activity, that is, sacking and dividing up the city of Jerusalem (v. 11). A poignant question implied by the arrangement of verses 10 and 11 is: How can you, the "brother," become "one of them," the "aliens"?

Additional details of Edom's behavior during the destruction of Jerusalem imply active participation. They are presented in a series of present-tense protests for what has already occurred. This literary device highlights the sense of irony for the future situation of Edom (vv. 12-14). Although the injunctions repeat sacking the city (v. 13), the more malicious activities are mocking the calamity of "your brother" (v. 12) and hindering the escape of refugees (v. 14).

Judgment upon the Nations

¹⁵For near is the day of the LORD
    for all the nations!
As you have done, so shall it be done to
    you,
    your deed shall come back upon your
    own head;

¹⁶As you have drunk upon my holy
    mountain,
    so shall all the nations drink contin-
    ually.
Yes, they shall drink and swallow,
    and shall become as though they had
    not been.

15b Condemnation of Edom. This statement, which is derived from the traditional Jewish practice of *lex talionis* (an eye for an eye), is the climax to Part One. It summarizes the judgment of retribution against Edom: "As you have done, so shall it be done to you" (see Exod 21:23-25; Lev 24:17-22).

PART TWO: ORACLES ABOUT THE DAY OF THE LORD

Obad 15a, 16-21

The relationship between Part One and Part Two is parallel to the Book of Joel. The plague of locusts in Part One of that book was a foreshadowing of the day of the Lord in Part Two. Similarly, in Obadiah, the anti-Edom oracles in Part One are a foreshadowing of the day of the Lord in Part Two. In addition, the different consequences of the day of the Lord are identical: punishment for the nations (especially Edom) and restoration for Judah (compare Joel 4:1-21 [3:1-21]; Obad 15a, 16-21).

Was one book the model for the other? Since Joel 4:17 [3:17] quotes Obad 17, he may have used the Obadian model with some editorial activity. It is also possible that both books are dependent on earlier traditions that they modified according to a similar structure. Some commentators consider the structure of a communal lamentation to be another convincing parallel for Joel and Obadiah.

15a, 16 Judgment of the nations. The imminent day of the Lord is announced for "all the nations" (v. 15a). The proclamation connects the previous section (vv. 11-14), where the phrase "on the day" was used ten times to detail the guilt of Edom. The proclamation also introduces the prominent theme of the present section (vv. 15a, 16-21).

Verse 16 indicates how the punishment of the nations is related to God's judgment of Judah and Edom. Again, the *lex talionis* is operative: "As you have drunk . . . so shall all the nations drink continually" (vv. 16a, 15b). The metaphor of drinking refers to the cup of God's judgment and wrath (see Jer 25:15-29). Just as the community experienced the bitterness of God's judgment "upon my holy mountain" (Jerusalem) in 586 B.C.E., so all the na-

Judah Shall Be Restored

[17]But on Mount Zion there shall be a portion saved;
the mountain shall be holy,

And the house of Jacob shall take possession
of those that dispossessed them.
[18]The house of Jacob shall be a fire,

tions (including Edom) will drink the cup until they "shall become as though they had not been" (v. 16b; compare Jer 50:25-28; Joel 3:4–4:21 [2:31–3:21]).

17-18 Return and restoration of Israel. The nations' judgment (vv. 15a, 16) is contrasted with Israel's future. Jacob (Judah) and Mount Zion (Jerusalem) are emphasized in restoration images (v. 17) corresponding to Joel's vision (Joel 4:17 [3:17]). A "portion" ("those that escape" in the Revised Standard Version) develops the theme of the "remnant" who would escape God's judgment (see Isa 4:3; 37:32; Zeph 2:7-9). Holiness characterizes the group.

Although confirming the tradition of Judah's restoration, Obadiah inserts a new perspective. The prophet includes the *whole* country by referring to Jacob *and* Joseph, who represent Judah and northern Israel respectively (v. 18a). All will share in the possession of Mount Zion. The fate of Esau (Edom) and the other nations symbolized by Esau is quite different. They will not survive (v. 18; compare Joel 1:4, 19; 2:3, 5). The metaphors of "fire" ("flame") and "stubble" indicate God's judgment against the nations through Israel's agency (see Isa 10:17; 29:5-6; Ezek 25:14). Again, the divine formula confirms the judgment (v. 18b; see vv. 4, 8).

19-21 Appendix: Return and restoration of Israel. The additional verses identify the day of the Lord as a day of great blessings for all the people of Israel. The participation of the nations appears to be limited to loss of land. Verse 21, however, suggests a different role.

The appendix outlines the extensive restoration of the boundaries of Israel. Unlike the small territory to which the Judeans returned in 538 B.C.E., their future homeland implies territorial boundaries greater than the ones achieved by King David (vv. 19-20). Precise geographical locations, however, are difficult to establish, since the Hebrew text is obscure. The major emphasis of verses 19 and 20 is to claim for Israel more land than it had possessed before deportations.

The role of Jacob, who "shall take possession of those that dispossessed them" (v. 17b), parallels "occupy," which occurs five times (vv. 19-20). The verbs suggest, in language reminiscent of covenant promises (see Gen 12:7; Exod 3:8; 2 Sam 7:10), how Israel will be restored.

"They shall occupy the Negeb, the mount of Esau" (v. 19a): The Negeb, an area south of Judah, was occupied by the Edomites during their collaboration with Babylon. It is identified by the name Idumea during the rule of

and the house of Joseph a flame;
The house of Esau shall be stubble,
and they shall set them ablaze and
devour them;
Then none shall survive of the house of
Esau,
for the LORD has spoken.

[19]They shall occupy the Negeb, the
mount of Esau,
and the foothills of the Philistines;
And they shall occupy the lands of
Ephraim
and the lands of Samaria,
and Benjamin shall occupy Gilead.

Herod the Great. The area is mentioned twice (vv. 19a; 20b) as an inclusion to highlight Israel's restoration as the reversal of Edomite fortune.

Instead of "They shall occupy . . . the foothills of the Philistines," the Revised Standard Version reads: "those of the Shephelah [shall possess] the land of the Philistines" (v. 19a). The Shephelah is a foothill region west of Judah and east of the Philistine coastland. Repossessing the territory of a traditional enemy, the Philistines, is one characteristic of restoration (see 1 Sam 17; Judg 13–16; 1 Sam 31:8-13; 2 Sam 21:15-22).

Ephraim, with its capital Samaria, is a region north of Jerusalem whose traditions are associated with northern Israel. This land, too, will be reclaimed. Benjamin is a territory north of Jerusalem that extends east to the Jordan River. Its inhabitants will extend borders to Gilead, a region northeast of Ephraim and across the Jordan (v. 19b).

Exiles of Israel were scattered in distant regions. Their identity and the geographical locations mentioned in verse 20 are disputed. The first group mentioned is "the captives of this host," which the Revised Standard Version translates "the exiles in Halah" (v. 20a). They may be deportees of northern Israel who were sent to Halah, a city northwest of Nineveh (see 2 Kgs 17:6). The group will occupy "Canaanite" ("Phoenician" in the Revised Standard Version) land along the Mediterranean coast, including the city of Zarephath near the coast, about ten miles south of Sidon (see 1 Kgs 17:9-24; Luke 4:26).

"The captives of Jerusalem" (v. 20b) parallels "the captives of this host" (v. 20a). Some deportees who did not return to rebuild Jerusalem are living in Sepharad. The identity of this city is disputed. Some suggest Babylon as a parallel to Halah, which is located there; others identify it with Sardis in Asia Minor (see Rev 3:1). Several Jewish commentators identify the term as Spain. Most recently it has been identified as Hesperides on the northern coast of Africa. Whatever the precise designation of Sepharad, the verse indicates that exiles far removed from Jerusalem will return to closer proximity by occupying "the cities of the Negeb."

Verse 21 forms an inclusion with verse 17 by returning attention to Mount Zion. Who will exercise dominion on Mount Zion and the mount of Esau

²⁰The captives of this host of the children
of Israel
shall occupy the Canaanite land as far
as Zarephath,
And the captives of Jerusalem who are
in Sepharad
shall occupy the cities of the Negeb.
²¹And saviors shall ascend Mount Zion
to rule the mount of Esau,
and the kingship shall be the LORD's.

(Edom)? The Hebrew is translated here as "saviors" (v. 21a). The people of Israel will function as *judges* and as God's *viceroys* in the kingdom. Sovereignty belongs to God alone (v. 21b). Other scholars interpret the term as God's restoration of the remnant, that is, the people who are "saved." This distinction offers Israel participation in the universal kingship of God. Other nations, however, may ultimately experience God's saving action.

Conclusion

The meager status of the Book of Obadiah among the Minor Prophets has not been transformed by later generations. The text is not listed in a lectionary for reflection on the mystery of God and human response. It is neither utilized for catechetical or preaching events nor suggested for personal or communal prayer. In addition, the book is not generally recognized in extrabiblical literature or contemporary situations. Why, then, was it preserved in tradition?

Commentaries and articles on Obadiah emphasize questions regarding the dating of the text, archeological data, and literary composition. The religious message appears less important in comparison to these considerations. When the religious dimensions of the text are investigated, the results are similar to the analysis about the Book of Joel (see p. 32):

a) The book presents a widely attested Jewish tradition about the relationship of God and the community. Restoration of the land is a symbol of the restoration of a spiritual relationship. Some reflection about the present state of Israel is occasionally related to the same premise.

b) The function of Israel among the nations is to offer witness and an invitation to future possibilities. God's blessing (restoration) can be a sign that judgment (punishment) may not be the ultimate condition.

c) Confidence in God's sovereignty over the world is indicated through the oracles about Edom's punishment and Israel's restoration.

Obadiah's contribution to postexilic prophecy may appear to be a very limited and localized message. In style, too, its bitter invective against Edom may offend believers (although the verses parallel some of the psalms and oracles against other nations).

Nonetheless, Obadiah can be read *in context* as a passionate plea to the God whose sovereignty assures Israel a future. Recourse to this God demands strong faith. The experience of the Exile and the prospect of return have not restored confidence in God nor in the community's self-image. Where else can the community turn? Only this God will forgive and restore Israel. Even more unexpectedly, this God will bless Jacob's (Israel's) estranged brother, Esau (Edom). An invitation will be extended to participate in the universal kingdom of the sovereign Lord.

The Book of Haggai

Introduction

Authorship

For the Books of Joel and Obadiah the author's identification was limited to the superscription of each book (v. 1). Additional biographical information was obtained through inferences in the text. For the Book of Haggai, however, there are more citations. The name Haggai appears eight times (1:1, 3, 13; 2:1, 10, 13, 14, 20).

The superscription (1:1) identifies his function as a prophet and names the addressees to whom he proclaims the oracles. Four verses identify Haggai with the word "prophet" and a traditional prophetic formula, "the word of the Lord came to . . ." (1:1, 3; 2:1, 10). Two verses identify Haggai as a "messenger of the Lord [proclaiming] the message of the Lord" (1:13; 2:20). Two verses mention his name as one who proclaims God's oracles (2:13, 14). The absence of any genealogy may be intended to emphasize Haggai's prophetic authority. Outside the text that bears his name, Haggai is linked with Zechariah as a prophet (see Ezra 5:1, 16; 6:14).

The name Haggai means "festival." Other names in the Old Testament are also derived from the same Hebrew root (see Gen 46:16; Num 26:15; 2 Sam 3:4; 1 Chr 3:2). The name may refer to the day of the prophet's birth, that is, a festival. It may designate Haggai's task of restoring the temple for cultic activities that celebrate festivals. While some identify Haggai as a priest, there is no indication in the text for this designation. It is preferable to associate him with cult prophets in Jerusalem. His position in that group, however, is unclear.

Dating of the text

The Books of Joel and Obadiah are difficult to date for three reasons: (a) their different positions in the Jewish and Alexandrian canons; (b) the absence of chronological data in the superscriptions; (c) minimal contextual clues. The dating process for the Book of Haggai presents an opposite situation: (a) an identical position in the canons; (b) clear chronological data in the superscription; (c) five precisely dated oracles.

The Book of Haggai is listed as the tenth Minor Prophet, between Zephaniah and Zechariah in both canons. The superscription and the chronological data of the text indicate that the ministry of Haggai included five proclamations of the word of the Lord from August through December 520 B.C.E.

The addressees are members of the second group of exiles from Babylon, who returned to Jerusalem about 522 B.C.E. under the leadership of Zerubbabel, the governor, and Joshua, the high priest. These two had been appointed to the positions of leadership during the early reign of Darius I of Persia (1:1; see pp. 9, 10).

The duration of Haggai's ministry is unclear. Although he is believed to have been a contemporary of Zechariah, there is no acknowledgement in either book of the other's activity. The recorded oracles indicate Haggai's perspective on how to achieve restoration for the Judean temple-community. The final form of the text indicates additional perspectives by the editor. The final date of the text is considered a question of secondary importance among commentators.

Composition of the text

For more than a century questions about the unity of the Book of Haggai have been discussed. The literary relationship between Haggai and Ezra has also been analyzed. More recently, the process of editorial activity has been examined for additional literary forms as well as for the religious significance of the oracles.

Scholars focus attention on one section of the text (2:10-19) in particular. Rearrangement of chapter 2 has been suggested as a partial solution to the difficulties of the verses. The New English Bible prefers this order: 1:14, 15, 13; 2:15-19, 10-14, 1-9, 20-23. Others, including the New American Bible, suggest that 2:15-19 should go after chapter 1. Revision of 2:18 is indicated by brackets. The editors believe that the date of the month is a gloss or that the date should be changed from the ninth month to the sixth month. None of the proposed rearrangements is confirmed in any text or version.

In general, there is a consensus about the structure, which provides a unity to the text, namely, five oracles introduced by editorial frameworks (see p. 13).

Outline of the book

PART ONE:	Reconstruction of the Temple (1:1-15a)
1:1	Superscription
1:2-11	First Oracle: Exhortation to Rebuild the Temple
1:12-15a	Second Oracle: Response and Assurance
PART TWO:	Future Glory of the Temple (1:15b–2:23)
1:15b–2:9	Third Oracle: Assurance and Promises
2:10-19	Fourth Oracle: Decisions and Future Blessings
2:20-23	Fifth Oracle: Future of Zerubbabel

The Book of Haggai

Text and Commentary

1 **Exhortation To Rebuild the Temple of the Lord.** ¹On the first day of the sixth month in the second year of King Darius, the word of the LORD came through the prophet Haggai to the governor of Judah, Zerubbabel, son of Shealtiel, and to the high priest Joshua, son of Jehozadak:

PART ONE: RECONSTRUCTION OF THE TEMPLE

Hag 1:1-15a

Part One offers a historical framework for the activity of Haggai by the insertion of chronological introductions and narrative detail. Another component of the oracles is the use of two traditional prophetic formulas: "Thus says the Lord of hosts" (1:2, 5, 7) and "says the Lord" (1:13). The contrast of prose introductions and poetic oracles is also apparent.

1:1 Superscription. This verse is not an introduction to the entire book of Haggai but is limited to the first oracle (1:2-11). In addition to mention of the date of August 520 B.C.E., the verse identifies the current Persian ruler, Darius I. Since the position of monarch no longer existed for the Jewish community after the Exile, the superscription accommodated the new situation by substituting the name of the foreign ruler.

Zerubbabel and Joshua, the appointed representatives of Darius' government, are the addressees of the first oracle. Their names are repeated in the second and third oracles. Unlike Haggai, both are identified by function *and genealogy:* "the governor of Judah, Zerubbabel, son of Shealtiel, and the high priest Joshua, son of Jehozadak."

Zerubbabel was the nephew of King Jehoiachin, who had been exiled to Babylon in 597 B.C.E. (see 1 Chr 3:17-19). His civic appointment was probably considered a minor position in the extensive Persian empire. In this early stage of restoration, however, his presence was a reminder of the royal Davidic household that had ruled in Jerusalem. Symbolically, he may have been a catalyst for dreams of rebuilding a new kingdom according to the model of the preexilic monarchy (see Hag 2:20-23).

Joshua is named Jeshua in the Books of Ezra and Nehemiah. He was a grandson of the chief priest in Jerusalem. Joshua and his father had been ex-

²Thus says the LORD of hosts: This people says: "Not now has the time come to rebuild the house of the LORD." ³ (Then this word of the LORD came through Haggai, the prophet:) ⁴Is it time for you to dwell in your own paneled houses, while this house lies in ruins? ⁵Now thus says the LORD of hosts: Consider your ways! ⁶You have sown much, but have brought

iled to Babylon (see 1 Chr 5:40-41). The designation "high priest" occurs here for the first time. As the religious leader of the returned exiles, his position may have been more autonomous. After him priestly authority became more significant (see pp. 10–11).

1:2-11 First oracle: Exhortation to rebuild the temple. The oracle consists of three sections related to the problem of temple restoration (vv. 2-4, 5-6, 7-11). Each is introduced by a traditional prophetic formula.

The first section (vv. 2-4) considers the question of the community's attitude toward rebuilding the temple. The initial statement is presented as a quotation from the community: "Not now has the time come to rebuild the house of the Lord" (v. 2). Next, a rhetorical question offers an opportunity to reflect on experience: "Is it time for you to dwell in your own paneled houses, while this house lies in ruins?" (v. 4).

It is clear that the entire community, not just the civic and religious leadership, is being challenged. The repetition of the word "time" (vv. 2, 4) draws attention to the irony of the situation. Who really decides what is the propitious "time" for rebuilding?

In preexilic tradition an interesting parallel suggests a response to the question. God provides the perspective. Recall the encounter between God and David *before* the first temple was constructed. In that situation David confided his worries to Nathan about a dwelling for God since he, David, lived in a house of cedar (2 Sam 7:2-3). God replied by promising to build David a house! The metaphor of "house" symbolized an everlasting dynasty and kingdom (2 Sam 7:7-17).

Why was Haggai's community waiting to rebuild the temple (v. 2)? The foundations for the temple had been laid in the spring of 536 B.C.E. by the first group that had returned from Babylon (see Ezra 3:7-13). No additional progress, however, had been achieved. What factors impeded the project? Had the community forgotten the edict of Cyrus for the task of restoration? Were the living conditions enervating? Did they experience opposition inside and outside the community? (See p. 9.) Perhaps they were waiting for the literal fulfillment of Jeremiah's prophecy: "Only after seventy years have elapsed for Babylon will I visit you and fulfill for you my promise to bring you back to this place" (Jer 29:10; 25:11; compare Zech 1:12, 16-17). If so, a few years still remain for the fulfillment. There is no specific reason

47

in little;
you have eaten, but have not been satisfied;
You have drunk, but have not been exhilarated;
have clothed yourselves, but not been warmed;
And he who earned wages
earned them for a bag with holes in it.

7   Thus says the LORD of hosts:
Consider your ways!
8   Go up into the hill country;
bring timber, and build the house
That I may take pleasure in it
and receive my glory, says the LORD.

9You expected much, but it came to little;
and what you brought home, I blew away.
For what cause? says the LORD of hosts.
Because my house lies in ruins,
while each of you hurries to his own house.

10Therefore the heavens withheld from you their dew,
and the earth her crops.
11And I called for a drought
upon the land and upon the mountains;

indicated in the text to account for the community's resistance to rebuilding the temple.

The second section, too, invites the community to reflect on its experience (vv. 5-6). "Consider your ways" (vv. 5b, 7b) introduces a series of comparisons between efforts at reconstituting daily living and the results. Although they have labored for food, drink, clothing, and wages, the results are meager and unsatisfying (v. 6).

The third section consists of a command and a judgment from God (vv. 7-11). It indicates the relationship between God's activity and the present experience of the community. The community must obtain timber to build the house of God (v. 8a). The urgency of the task consists in giving glory to God (v. 8b).

The expectations about restoration cannot be met (v. 9a). Why? God has entered into the situation. Efforts are useless, especially in providing homes for themselves while God's house "lies in ruins" (v. 9b). Stark living conditions are the direct result of God's initiative for the drought. The land and its produce, persons and their livestock are affected (vv. 10-11).

The literary form of verses 9-11 is a question-answer pattern. The didactic style of the verses repeats the plight of the community (vv. 4-6). In addition, it emphasizes the need for immediate response on the part of the community. Clearly, the temple must be rebuilt. However, the physical restoration suggests a metaphorical function.

According to Haggai, to rebuild the temple means to restore the relationship of the community with God (compare the commentary on Joel 1:5-20, p. 19). Restoration of God's house is the primary responsibility of the community. Until the task is completed, the community lives under God's judgment enacted through the Exile and continuing in the harsh conditions of

Upon the grain, and upon the wine, and upon the oil,
and upon all that the ground brings forth;
Upon men and upon beasts,
and upon all that is produced by hand.

¹²Then Zerubbabel, son of Shealtiel, and the high priest Joshua, son of Jehozadak, and all the remnant of the people listened to the voice of the Lord, their God, and to the words of the prophet Haggai, because the Lord, their God, had sent him, and the people feared because of the Lord. ¹³And the Lord's messenger, Haggai, proclaimed to the people as the message of the Lord: I am with you, says the Lord.

¹⁴Then the Lord stirred up the spirit of the governor of Judah, Zerubbabel, son of Shealtiel, and the spirit of the high priest Joshua, son of Jehozadak, and the spirit of all the remnant of the people, so that they came and set to work on the house of the Lord of hosts, their God, ¹⁵on the twenty-fourth day of the sixth month.

their lives. When the temple is completed, blessing will replace judgment. The Lord will dwell in the temple-community again.

1:12-15a Second oracle: Response and assurance. The ordering of the verses is debated (see p. 45). The dating for the oracle does not follow the pattern of the other oracles, that is, a prose introduction (see 1:1; 1:15b–2:1; 2:10, 18, 20). For some commentators, the dating information at the conclusion of the oracle (v. 15) indicates the need for rearrangement. They suggest that the phrase "on the twenty-fourth day of the sixth month" ought to be shifted to 2:15 to provide a chronology for the third oracle (2:15-19). Rearrangement, however, is not necessary.

The prose reflection of verse 12 indicates the importance of Haggai's position in the temple-community. The editor of the text draws attention to his prophetic credentials (vv. 12b-13; see p. 44). In addition, Haggai's proclamation is obeyed by the entire community. "All the remnant of the people" may be inserted to identify the returned exiles as the ones who will receive the blessings of restoration (v. 12a; 2:2; see Isa 10:20-22; Mic 4:7; Zech 8:6, 11-12). This group "listened to the voice of the Lord" (see Jer 23:3; Deut 6:2-3).

The brief oracle is located in the center of the editorial comment (v. 13). "I am with you" is a traditional proclamation of assurance (see Gen 28:15; Exod 3:12; Jer 1:8; 30:10-11; Isa 41:10; 43:5). Here the word is accompanied by action as the Lord "stirs up" the spirit of Zerubbabel, Joshua, and the community for the task of rebuilding the temple (v. 14). The Hebrew verb from which the word for "spirit" is derived is used to describe God's power to activate Cyrus, who authorized the exiles to return (2 Chr 36:22-23) and to activate the exiles themselves (Ezra 1:5).

The phrase "twenty-fourth day of the sixth month" (v. 15a) does not have to be shifted to another place in the text. The date recalls to the community

49

2 **Future Glory of the New Temple.** In the second year of King Darius, ¹on the twenty-first day of the seventh month, the word of the LORD came through the prophet Haggai: ²Tell this to the governor of Judah, Zerubbabel, son of Shealtiel, and to the high priest Joshua, son of Jehozadak, and to the remnant of the people:
³Who is left among you
    that saw this house in its former
    glory?

the process involved in their own call to rebuild the temple. Having listened to the proclamations of Haggai (vv. 2-11), they determined to be obedient. God's subsequent word and action of assurance (vv. 13-14) encouraged their response to be faithful. They began the project of restoring the temple.

PART TWO: FUTURE GLORY OF THE TEMPLE

Hag 1:15b-2:23

Part Two refers to future blessings for the Judean temple-community, blessings that were proclaimed before the Exile. It offers hope in present circumstances, blessings for the future, and a role of prominence to Zerubbabel, the civic leader. Four identical structural components link the two parts of the book: chronological introductions; addressees; question-and-answer pattern; assurances. Promises of future blessings are a development of the Lord's assurances (vv. 6-9, 21-23).

1:15b-2:9 Third oracle: Assurance and promises. The chronological introduction (1:15b-2:1) follows the pattern of the first oracle (1:1). The "twenty-first day of the seventh month" indicates nearly one month of work on rebuilding the temple. The date is also important in the Jewish calendar: it is the final day of a week's celebration of the feast of Booths, during which the community would remember its ancestors' living in tents as they journeyed through the wilderness (see Lev 23:33-36, 39-43; Deut 16:13-15). As one of the three pilgrimage feasts (along with Passover and Pentecost), the feast of Booths would draw crowds to Jerusalem.

The addressees of the third oracle are identical with those of the previous oracle: Zerubbabel, Joshua, and the "remnant of the people" (v. 2). Haggai may have chosen the occasion of the festival because of the presence of the civic and religious leaders and other persons gathered in Jerusalem. The celebration provided an association with the period of the first temple. During Solomon's reign the temple had been dedicated on this festival (see 1 Kgs 8; compare Ezek 45:25; Zech 14:16).

The question-and-answer pattern (1:9-11) continues in the first section of the oracle (2:3-5). A series of three questions (v. 3) invites those assembled to reflect on their memories of the temple before Babylon conquered Jerusa-

And how do you see it now?
Does it not seem like nothing in your eyes?
⁴But now take courage, Zerubbabel, says the LORD,
and take courage, Joshua, high priest, son of Jehozadak,
And take courage, all you people of the land,
says the LORD, and work!
For I am with you, says the LORD of hosts.

⁵This is the pact that I made with you when you came out of Egypt,
And my spirit continues in your midst; do not fear!
⁶ For thus says the LORD of hosts:
One moment yet, a little while,
and I will shake the heavens and the earth,
the sea and the dry land.
⁷I will shake all the nations,
and the treasures of all the nations will come in,

lem with the probable assistance of Edom (see the commentary on Obadiah, p. 34). The comparison of the Solomonic temple and the sporadic progress of reconstruction since 538 B.C.E. left no doubt about which was a glorious achievement.

A proclamation of assurances links the third oracle to the second oracle. While recorded briefly in the second oracle (1:13), the declaration occurs in an expanded form (2:4-5). Officials and community members are exhorted to "take courage" (three times), and not to fear (v. 4). The Lord is present; God's spirit dwells in all the members of the community (v. 5b; see 1:14).

The traditional language of assurance is developed by an editor in verse 5a. The reference to God's relationship with Israel provides a continuity of experience for the returned exiles. The specific event, "the pact," is the covenant experience at Mount Sinai. "I am with you, says the Lord of hosts" is assurance to both groups (v. 4b; see Exod 29:45-46).

The second section of the oracle announces future blessings for the community (vv. 6-9). The uncertainty of when they will be fulfilled is indicated by "one moment yet, a little while" (v. 6a). The Revised Standard Version, however, interprets the phrase to mean that God will act again in a similar way: "once again, in a little while."

While cosmic shaking is attributed to God in earlier traditions (see Amos 8:8-9; Isa 2:13-21; 13:13; Ezek 38:20; compare Joel 2:10; 4:16 [3:16]), the proclamation here promises a new reality (vv. 6b-7a). The "nations" and their "treasures" will be shaken, too. There is no indication in this verse of "universalism," that is, universal salvation, as some commentators have suggested. They compare this section to Isa 60:5-11, which presents a different concept.

The future action of God will be directed to filling the new temple with "glory" (v. 7b). "Silver" and "gold" from Babylon and the nations will be used for sacred vessels to worship God in glory (v. 8; compare Zech 6:9-15). The Lord's direct intervention, then, will accomplish what no dedicated

And I will fill this house with glory,
  says the LORD of hosts.
⁸Mine is the silver and mine the gold,
  says the LORD of hosts.
⁹Greater will be the future glory of this
  house
    than the former, says the LORD of
    hosts;
And in this place I will give peace,
  says the LORD of hosts!

Offerings of the Unclean Rejected.
¹⁰On the twenty-fourth day of the ninth
month, in the second year of King Darius,
the word of the LORD came to the prophet
Haggai: ¹¹Thus says the LORD of hosts:
Ask the priests for a decision: ¹²If a man
carries sanctified flesh in the fold of his
garment and the fold touches bread, or
pottage, or wine, or oil, or any other
food, do they become sanctified? "No,"

human effort could accomplish independently. Greater glory will be in the Lord's second temple than in the period of the first temple (v. 9a). The present situation of the community will be reversed.

The section concludes with a comprehensive promise of blessings, "peace" (shalom) in verse 9b (compare Zech 8:12, 19). What constitutes "peace"? Where is it to be located? For whom? The term's multiple interpretation transcends any particular designation. The verse may be intentionally unclear in the Hebrew text. In the Greek text, however, a scribe appended a reflection: "and peace of soul as a possession for all who build, to erect this temple."

2:10-19 Fourth oracle: Decisions and future blessings. This oracle is the most difficult passage to interpret. Commentators debate virtually every perspective: dating indications; the connection between verses 11-14 and 15-19; the placement of the oracle; the addressees (v. 14); the religious significance of the passage. The division of the oracle into two sections (vv. 10-14 and 15-19) is generally agreed upon among scholars.

Verse 10 identifies the date for the oracle (compare v. 18). There are several suggestions about altering the date and the placement of the oracle (see p. 45). Rearrangement, however, is not necessary, since precise dating is not the only factor to be considered for interpretation. The verse indicates that a few months after work had commenced on the temple, Haggai proclaimed another oracle.

In the first section of the oracle, the initial statement in verse 11 exhorts Haggai to consult the "priests" for a "decision" (torah). Priests were the arbitrators for all circumstances of daily life (see Deut 17:8-13; compare Zech 7:2-3; Mal 2:7). Each decision under their jurisdiction was connected with the primary concern of the community: What constitutes holiness, that is, what is involved in purity and defilement? The verses describe a set of circumstances about ritual purity. The situation is formulated in two question-and-answer patterns (vv. 12-13; see 1:9-11; 2:3-5).

The first question is about "sanctified flesh," or roasted meat that had been blessed for ritual sacrifice (v. 12). If a person were carrying the ritual

the priests answered. [13]Then Haggai said: If a person unclean from contact with a corpse touches any of these, do they become unclean? The priests answered, "They become unclean." [14]Then Haggai continued:

So is this people, and so is this nation
in my sight, says the LORD:
And so are all the works of their hands;
and what they offer there is unclean.

Promise of Immediate Blessings. [15]But now, consider from this day forward. Before there was a stone laid upon a stone in the temple of the LORD, [16]how did you fare?

When one went to a heap of grain for
twenty measures,
it would yield but ten;
When another went to the vat to draw
fifty measures,
there would be but twenty.

element, would the element effect holiness for other objects that came into contact with it? The priests respond negatively. Holiness is not transferred by contact with a sacred object (compare Exod 29:37; 30:29; Lev 6:26-27).

Another perspective of the first question follows (v. 13). If a person is defiled because of contact with an unclean object, would the defilement be transferred to other objects with which the person comes into contact (see Lev 6:20-21, 25-28; 11:24-28; 22:4-7)? The priests respond positively. Defilement, unlike holiness, is easily transferable. Contemporary sociological analysis of Jewish purity and defilement codes confirms the extraordinary stratification implicit in groups, religious responsibilities, and possibilities of changing one's status of purity and defilement.

The climax of the section occurs in verse 14. It states the judgment of the Lord following the norms of the priests' decisions. To whom is the judgment directed? To "this people . . . this nation." What is the verdict? "All the works of their hands, and what they offer there is unclean." The identity of the addressees and the judgment of the Lord provide the religious significance of the section.

Earlier scholarship suggested that the addressees were the Samaritans or a group later reinterpreted as the Samaritans. According to Ezra, their offer to collaborate with the returned exiles in the restoration of the temple had been spurned. During the leadership of Zerubbabel and Joshua, the Samaritans retaliated, and progress on the temple was hampered (see Ezra 4:1-5). Although the chronology in Ezra is uncertain, the events are part of a reliable tradition. As enemies of Judah, their history indicted them as "unclean." The offerings of the Samaritans would also be defiled.

Contemporary scholarship, however, does not accept the identification of the Samaritans. It prefers to identify the addressees as the temple-community of Judah because (a) the only group that Haggai addresses throughout the book is the returned exiles; (b) the term "this people" refers to the community (see 1:2a); (c) the terms "this people, this nation" are used

53

¹⁷I struck you in all the works of your
     hands
  with blight, searing wind, and hail,
     yet you did not return to me, says the
     LORD.
¹⁸[Consider from this day forward:
from the twenty-fourth day of the ninth
month. From the day on which the temple
of the LORD was founded, consider!]
¹⁹Indeed, the seed has not sprouted,
     nor have the vine, the fig, the pome-
        granate
  and the olive tree yet borne.
From this day, I will bless!

in prophetic literature to designate Judah in judgments of reproach (see Jer 6:19, 21; 14:10, 11).

What is the indictment against the temple-community? Commentators do not agree. Six interpretations represent the discussion:

a) The phrase "the works of their hands" refers to the yield from agriculture and animals. No ritual offerings are acceptable, because the altar has not been sanctified. Although it is unclear whether the altar was destroyed in 586 B.C.E. (compare 2 Kgs 25; Ezek 43:13-26), restoration of the temple would include a rededication of the altar. Thus Haggai is exhorting the community to attend to the appropriate cleansing of the altar while the work of restoration continues.

b) A similar interpretation proposes that the temple itself may be identified with "sanctified flesh" (v. 12a). Until the temple is restored, the community remains unclean.

c) A third interpretation suggests that the ritual offerings are a symbol of the community's life. Since the group has failed to live according to God's covenant, the offerings are unclean (compare Isa 57:3-10; 65:3-7). The offerings will be acceptable if the community reforms (see Isa 1:15; compare Isa 33:14ff.; Ezek 18:5ff).

d) Israel had been chosen to be holy (see Exod 19:6), yet subsequent history indicated that it had become defiled. Only acceptance of God's blessings and repentance will redefine the community's status before God (see 2:19).

e) God's future presence in the temple (2:2-9) will not automatically assure that the community is ritually pure for worship. The temple and its ritual are not a guarantee of holiness. Repentance and integrity of life are necessary to give the ritual its context and meaning. This interpretation is based on an addition of the Greek text: "Because of their early profits, they shall be pained because of their toil, and you have hated those who reprove at the gates" (compare Amos 5:10). The addition is the earliest interpretation of the Hebrew text.

f) There is no indictment. Rather, "the works of their hands" refers to the reconstruction of the temple. It is the effort of the community to prepare

Pledge to Zerubbabel. ²⁰The message of the LORD came a second time to Haggai on the twenty-fourth day of the month: ²¹Tell this to Zerubbabel, the governor of Judah:

I will shake the heavens and the earth;
²² I will overthrow the thrones of kingdoms,
destroy the power of the kingdoms of the nations.

for the Lord's coming. When the temple is restored, God's presence will fill the temple with glory and renew the community (see Ezek 36:22-32; 43:1-9).

These various interpretations indicate a tension between God's initiative and human effort. They also present the importance of temple restoration and sacrificial worship as symbols of the condition of the community. Both perspectives link the temple-community with the collective experience of Israel. Both realities will continue in future communities.

Verse 15a provides a connection between the first and second sections of the oracle: "But now, consider from this day forward." The directive appeals to the community to reflect on its situation before the task of rebuilding had begun (vv. 15b-16a). The section repeats the comparison in the first oracle between human efforts and results as well as God's intervention (vv. 16b-17; see 1:5-7, 9-11). One new judgment occurs about the community's response to its stark situation: "you did not return to me" (v. 17b).

Although the section repeats the experience of the community, a new emphasis is apparent. Notice that "consider" occurs three times (vv. 15a, 18 [2 times]). The immediate object of the verb is "this day." It is not a reference to an indefinite day but to a precise day, that is, "the twenty-fourth day of the ninth month" (v. 18a). The significance of the date is specified: "a stone laid upon a stone in the temple of the Lord" (v. 15b) and "the temple of the Lord was founded" (v. 18b).

Some commentators propose that the verses identify the day on which the foundation stone of the temple was laid (compare Ezra 3:10-13; Zech 4:9). A sacred place for worship was restored. The formal ceremony of rededication is not described. Rather, the function of verses 15-19 is to compare the situation of the community before and after the event. Beforehand, the community experienced the judgment of God; afterward, however, God transformed judgment into blessing: "From this day, I will bless!" (v. 19b).

Other commentators suggest that the emphasis on "this day" is not directly related to the laying of the foundation stone. Rather, the oracle proclaimed on "this day" reveals the community's need for repentance. Blessing will follow judgment (see v. 17b) if the community returns to God.

2:20-23 Fifth oracle: Future of Zerubbabel. Verse 20 introduces the oracle with the same date as the previous one, which presented the Lord's judgment and blessing on the temple-community. The addressee is "Zerubbabel,

I will overthrow the chariots and their
    riders,
and the riders with their horses
shall go down by one another's
    sword.
²³ On that day, says the LORD of hosts,

I will take you, Zerubbabel,
    son of Shealtiel, my servant, says the
    LORD,
And I will set you as a signet ring;
    for I have chosen you, says the LORD
    of hosts.

the governor of Judah" (v. 21a). The proclamation contrasts the treatment of the nations—judgment (v. 22)—with that of Zerubbabel and the community—blessing (v. 23).

From 522 to 520 B.C.E. Darius I struggled to achieve stability among the rebelling satrapies of the Persian empire (see p. 9). The situation may have been interpreted as a fortuitous one for Judah to achieve political independence as another dimension of restoration. Zerubbabel as a Davidic descendant would restore the hopes of the returned exiles as well as promote the fulfillment of messianic expectations.

The introduction to God's action repeats the cosmic shaking of the third oracle (v. 21b; compare 2:6b). Verse 22 identifies God's action upon Judah's enemies: "overthrow," "destroy," "go down." The terms are found in the Torah and the Prophets to describe the Sodom and Gomorrah tradition (Gen 19:25, 29; Deut 29:23; Amos 4:11); in oracles against the nations (Isa 13:19; 23:11; Jer 51:20-21); and in the Exodus from Egypt (see Exod 14:23; 15:1, 5). There is no indication in the verse of when God will act on behalf of Judah.

Verse 23 describes God's action toward Zerubbabel "on that day." The verbs and titles identify Zerubbabel with other figures who were particularly chosen by God. The first action and title are presented in verse 23a: "I will take you" indicates a special election (see Exod 6:7; Josh 24:3; 2 Sam 7:8). "My servant" assigns Zerubbabel another responsibility to his position as governor. The role especially identified David (2 Sam 7:5; 1 Kgs 11:32, 36; 1 Chr 17:4; Ps 132:10; Ezek 34:23; 37:24-25), Judah, and Mount Zion (Ps 78:68-70).

"I will set you as a signet ring" is the second promise of God to Zerubbabel (v. 23b; see Sir 49:11). The proclamation is a reversal of the one to Jeconiah (Coniah), Zerubbabel's grandfather, just before the Exile: "As I live, says the Lord, if you, Coniah, son of Jehoiakim, king of Judah, are a signet ring on my right hand, I will snatch you from it" (Jer 22:24).

The signet ring contained the king's seal, which was used to stamp important documents with royal approval. The ring is a metaphor to indicate the relationship of the king to God. The king functioned as God's representative. The final phrase of verse 23 appears to confirm the possibility of Zerubbabel's attaining royal status: "for I have chosen you, says the Lord of hosts."

Conclusion

The Book of Haggai has been analyzed according to the perspective of unfulfilled prophecy. Images of restoration were proclaimed during the Exile to revitalize hope (see Ezek 40–48; Isa 40–55). The experiences of the first groups of returnees from Babylon did not correspond to the prophetic oracles. Haggai's contribution about a restored temple and a reconstituted ruler of Davidic ancestry (2:1-9, 20-23) were realized neither in his own lifetime nor in the lifetimes of future communities.

Perhaps the apparent "failure" of Haggai's proclamations accounts for the minimal value given to his book by several commentators. Some commentators, however, assess the value of the book differently. Canonical critics, in particular, present the contribution of Haggai for succeeding generations. It is important to consider his message for contemporaries and for future believers.

Attending to probable expectations of both groups, one can analyze Haggai's understanding of God's revelation:

a) Haggai's directives to the community addressed both dimensions of restoration, that is, a restored temple and a reconstituted Davidic ruler. He urged the people forward in the immediate task of rebuilding the temple. The process, in turn, facilitated their identity with God as a temple-community. He also warned them that their identity consisted in integrity of life as well as prescribed ritual sacrifice to confirm their covenant relationship with God.

b) Haggai reminded the community that their efforts at restoration would contribute to the fulfillment of visions proclaimed during the Exile. The community needed the motivation to connect their labor, which was so slow and hampered, to their past history and future possibilities.

c) Haggai did not propose that there was a simple relationship between the initiative of God and the response of the community; rather, he respected the mystery of the faithful God and the struggling community. Haggai was convinced that God would never abandon the community. He believed in the God who consistently enters into the human condition, filling it clearly, at times, with glory and presence.

The Book of Zechariah

Introduction

The introduction indicates that two centuries of political and religious history divide First Zechariah (chs. 1–8) and Second Zechariah (chs. 9–14). As a preparation for the study of Zechariah, then, it is helpful to review the information about First and Second Zechariah, especially the sections on historical background, attitudes and perspectives about reconstruction, and literary forms (see pp. 10–14). In addition, a comparison of the material on authorship, dating and composition of the text, and an outline of the texts will provide a clearer context for study of each section of Zechariah.

FIRST ZECHARIAH

(1:1–8:23)

Authorship

Unlike Haggai, whose name was supplemented only by his function (prophet), Zechariah is identified by function and genealogy. The superscription (1:1) and the introduction to the first vision (1:7) describe him as "the prophet Zechariah, son of Berechiah, son of Iddo." His identity as a prophet may be inferred from his name, which means "Yahweh has remembered." It occurs about thirty times in the Old Testament.

Outside the text that bears his name, Zechariah is identified with Haggai as a "prophet" and as the "son of Iddo" (see Ezra 5:1; 6:14). The phrase "son of Berechiah" (Zech 1:1, 7) is occasionally considered a gloss (see the note in the Jerusalem Bible; compare Matt 23:25). The phrase, however, may indicate Zechariah's father.

Iddo, the grandfather of Zechariah, was one of the priestly exiles returning from Babylon with Zerubbabel and Jeshua (Joshua; see Neh 12:4, 16). Consequently, some commentators emphasize Zechariah's priestly origin. Others identify him as a priest because of his concerns for the restoration of the temple and cult as well as the priesthood.

Dating of the text

First Zechariah, like Haggai, provides specific dates for oracles and visions. The book, which is found in the eleventh position in both canons, between Haggai and Malachi, is a postexilic text. Exact chronology is established for the beginning of Zechariah's ministry in the superscription: October-November 520 B.C.E., during the second year of Darius' reign (1:1). Zechariah's ministry began two months after Haggai proclaimed his first oracle (see Hag 1:1).

The second date suggests that Zechariah's ministry concluded two years later: November-December 518 B.C.E., during the fourth year of Darius' reign (7:1). Comparing the dates attributed to Haggai's ministry shows that Zechariah's ministry was eighteen months longer (see pp. 44–45).

The civic and religious leaders of the temple-community mentioned in Haggai appear also in First Zechariah: Zerubbabel (4:6-10; 6:11-14) and Joshua (3:1-10; 6:11-14). The addressees of Haggai and First Zechariah are identical, that is, the second group of returned exiles from Babylon.

Nothing in chapter 8 or in any editorial revisions indicates a later chronology for Zechariah's ministry. The final form of First Zechariah is not considered apart from the dating process of the entire text (fourteen chapters) and its canonical placement (see p. 89).

Composition of the text

Visions constitute the major literary genre of First Zechariah (1:7–6:15). They are interspersed with oracles, which function as responses. A separate collection of oracles (7:1–8:23) is also apparent. Additional material has expanded the visions and the oracles to constitute the final form of the text. The motive ordinarily given for the redactional activity is a changing political context.

Scholars discuss two questions about redaction: Who is responsible for the additions? What sources were used? The questions are part of the complex considerations of the relationship of Zechariah (chs. 1–14) to apocalyptic literature (see pp. 14–15). The relationship of First Zechariah to Second Zechariah regarding the editorial process of the book and the development of religious ideas is discussed below (see pp. 90, 106).

Rearrangement of the text is suggested for chapters 3 and 4. The Jerusalem Bible changes verses *within* the chapters: 3:1, 2, 3, 4a, 5, 4b, 6, 7, 9a, 8, 9b, 10; 4:1, 2, 3, 4, 5, 6a, 10b, 11, 12, 13, 14, 6b, 7, 8, 9, 10a. The New English Bible rearranges chapter 4 as frames around chapter 3: 4:1-3, 11-14; 3:1-10; 4:4-5, 6-10. Note that the New American Bible sequence of this commentary rearranges only chapter 4: 4:4-10, 1-3, 11-14. Rearrangement is one solution to the difficult task of interpreting First Zechariah.

The three-part structure of the text is recognized by most commentators: (a) introduction (1:1-6); (b) visions (1:7–6:15); (c) oracles about fasting and future days (7:1–8:23). Nonetheless, there is litte consensus about the interpretation of the visions and oracles. It is no wonder that several contemporary commentators concur with Jerome in their judgment of Zechariah as the most obscure book of the Bible.

Outline of the book

There are two places in the text of First Zechariah where the numbering of chapters and verses is different. This commentary, based on the New American Bible, represents the Hebrew text, while other Bibles and commentaries may use the Greek text. The chart compares the versions:

Hebrew Text	Greek Text
2:1-4	1:18-21
2:5-17	2:1-13

In this commentary the numbering of the Greek text is in brackets.

PART ONE:	Introduction to First Zechariah (1:1-6)
1:1	Superscription
1:2-6	Return to the Lord
PART TWO:	"Night" Visions and Responses (1:7–6:15)
1:7-12	First Vision: Equestrians
1:13-17	Responses
2:1-4[1:18-21]	Second Vision: Four Horns and Four Blacksmiths
2:5-9 [2:1-5]	Third Vision: Measuring Line
2:10-17 [2:6-13]	Responses
3:1-5	Fourth Vision: Joshua the High Priest
3:6-10	Responses
4:1-6a, 10b-14	Fifth Vision: Lampstand
4:6b-10a	Responses
5:1-4	Sixth Vision: Flying Scroll
5:5-11	Seventh Vision: Flying Bushel
6:1-8	Eighth Vision: Four Chariots
6:9-15	Responses and a Crown
PART THREE:	Oracles about Fasting and the Future (7:1–8:23)
7:1-3	Question about Fasting
7:4-7	Responses
7:8-14	Another Collection of Responses
8:1-8	Blessings for Jerusalem
8:9-17	Encouragement and Challenge for Jerusalem
8:18-23	Responses about Fasting and the Future

The Book of Zechariah

Text and Commentary

1 **Necessity of Conversion.** ¹In the second year of Darius, in the eighth month, the word of the LORD came to the prophet Zechariah, son of Berechiah, son of Iddo: ²The LORD was indeed angry with your fathers. . . . ³and say to them: Thus says the LORD of hosts: Return to me, says the LORD of hosts, and I will return to you, says the LORD of hosts. ⁴Be not like your fathers whom the former prophets warned: Thus says the LORD of hosts: Turn from your evil ways and from

PART ONE: INTRODUCTION TO FIRST ZECHARIAH

Zech 1:1-6

The introduction establishes a continuity between "your fathers" and the returned exiles. What the Judean prophets had proclaimed about God's imminent judgment had occurred in the destruction of Jerusalem. That experience is a mirror for the next generation who returned to rebuild Jerusalem.

1:1 Superscription. The verse is similar to the superscription of Haggai (see Hag 1:1). It identifies the Persian ruler (Darius I), the year and month, and confirms Zechariah's ministry as prophet.

While the superscription of Haggai emphasizes his prophetic credentials, Zechariah's focuses on a genealogy of a priestly family that survived the Exile. Whereas Haggai's oracle is addressed to the leaders of the temple-community and the returnees from Babylon (see Hag 1:1-2), Zechariah's oracle has no specific addressees (see Zech 1:2ff.); from the context it is inferred that it is addressed to members of the temple-community.

1:2-6 Return to the Lord. Verse 2 is an editorial insertion that interrupts the sequence of the prophetic oracle. The verse links the present generation of returned exiles to their relatives: "The Lord was indeed angry with your fathers. . . ." The connection between the two generations is continued by the repetition of "your fathers" (vv. 4, 5, 6; see Ezek 20:27, 30; Jer 7:25-26).

The divine formulas "Thus says the Lord of hosts" (vv. 3, 4) and "says the Lord" (vv. 3, 4) complete the prophetic formula introduced in verse 1. The title "Lord of hosts," which appears three hundred times in the Old Testament, occurs frequently in three prophets of this commentary (53 times in Zechariah; 14 times in Haggai; 24 times in Malachi).

your wicked deeds. But they would not listen or pay attention to me, says the LORD. ⁵Your fathers, where are they? And the prophets, can they live forever? ⁶But my words and my decrees, which I entrusted to my servants the prophets, did not these overtake your fathers? Then they repented and admitted: "The LORD of hosts has treated us according to our ways and deeds, just as he had determined he would."

The exhortation of the Lord of hosts is "Return to me" (v. 3a). Specific reasons for returning are not indicated (compare 2 Chr 30:6-9; Isa 44:22; Joel 2:12; Mal 3:7). The community, however, is assured that the Lord will return to them (v. 3b).

The exhortation is strengthened by reference to their ancestors' experience (v. 4a). Previous generations had refused to obey the Lord's warning proclaimed through the prophets (v. 4b). By not listening, the "fathers" refused to turn to the Lord (v. 4c).

The term "former prophets" refers to the preexilic prophets (see Jer 35:15). Later, in the Jewish canon, the term indicates a collection of books describing early prophetic activity in Israel (Josh; Judg; 1-2 Sam; 1-2 Kgs).

Verse 5 consists of two rhetorical questions about the existence of "your fathers" and the "prophets." Their mortality is compared with the eternal power of the Lord's "words and decrees" proclaimed by "my servants the prophets" (v. 6a). It is God's words that "overtake your fathers." The verb "overtake" indicates God's action to impart blessing (see Deut 28:2) or curse (Deut 28:15) on a community. Here the context favors "curse," that is, the destruction of Jerusalem.

The second half of verse 6, an editorial addition, refers to the current situation of Zechariah and the community. They have learned from the past that God is faithful to promises. They have accepted the invitation to return, to restore their relationship to God, to reconstruct the temple.

What does the language of the oracle suggest about Zechariah's function in the community? Zechariah may have used traditional prophetic formulas to strengthen his position in prophetic tradition. The authority of the "former prophets" appears to have nearly canonical status: what they proclaimed was fulfilled in the experience of the Exile. In this perspective Zechariah is continuing an old tradition and contributes nothing new to prophecy.

Zechariah's intent may be to appeal to a collective history and to invite the community to be unlike their ancestors, that is, to return to the Lord and rebuild the covenant relationship. The visions indicate dimensions of that choice. Zechariah builds on the past to create new possibilities for the future. The perspectives are not contradictory. The first represents older scholarship (see pp. 6–7), while the second indicates more recent scholarship.

The Four Horsemen. ⁷In the second year of Darius, on the twenty-fourth day of Shebat, the eleventh month, the word of the LORD came to the prophet Zechariah, son of Berechiah, son of Iddo, in the following way: ⁸I had a vision during the night. There appeared the driver of a red horse, standing among myrtle trees in a shady place, and behind him were red, sorrel, and white horses. ⁹Then I asked, "What are these, my lord?"; and the angel who spoke with me answered me, "I will show you what these are." ¹⁰The man who was standing among the myrtle trees spoke up and said, "These are they whom the LORD has sent to patrol the earth."

PART TWO: "NIGHT" VISIONS AND RESPONSES

Zech 1:7–6:15

The "night" visions of First Zechariah are regarded as some of the most difficult passages of the Old Testament. Basic questions that contemporary scholars discuss are: What is the specific function of the visions in regard to the ministry and message of Zechariah? What is the relationship of the visions and the accompanying oracles? What is the literary genre of the visions? Does the literary genre determine the religious message?

Visions are common in prophetic literature (see Isa 6; Ezek 1:1; Jer 1:11-19). The visions of First Zechariah, however, are generally identified with a distinctive literary genre called "apocalyptic." One characteristic of the genre is the presence of a secret revelation of God transmitted through a vision. The images of the vision are not taken literally; rather, each image is a symbol that is interpreted for its own value.

Ordinarily an angel assists in the interpretation of the vision. The Hebrew term for "angel" means "messenger." It is used in connection with many persons in the Old Testament. Even the phrase "messenger of the Lord" does not necessarily designate an angelic being. Prophets are identified with this phrase (see Hag 1:13; 2:20).

Other characteristics of apocalyptic literature are well-defined ideas about God, human beings, good, evil, and the world. Since the visions of First Zechariah are "apocalyptic" in form but not in content, scholars do not situate First Zechariah in that category. Some commentators designate the visions as "proto-apocalyptic."

The visions of First Zechariah may be symbolic representations of what is necessary for the restoration for the temple-community. Each vision generally follows a pattern: introductory statement; description; question about interpretation; the angel's explanation.

1:7-12 First vision: Equestrians. The superscription offers additional chronological data (v. 7). The month Shebat is from the Babylonian calendar adopted by the Jewish community after the Exile. The name that ap-

¹¹And they answered the angel of the LORD who was standing among the myrtle trees and said, "We have patrolled the earth; see, the whole earth is tranquil and at rest!"

¹²Then the angel of the Lord spoke out and said, "O LORD of hosts, how long will you be without mercy for Jerusalem and the cities of Judah that have felt your anger these seventy years?" ¹³To the angel who spoke with me, the LORD replied with comforting words.

¹⁴And the angel who spoke with me said to me, Proclaim: Thus says the LORD of hosts: I am deeply moved for the sake of Jerusalem and Zion, ¹⁵and I am exceed-

pears here does not occur anywhere else in the Old Testament. That detail and "the second year of Darius" place Zechariah's ministry during the Persian period. The visions occurred about three months after the first oracle addressed to Zechariah.

Verse 8a is an awkward transition between the "word" addressed to Zechariah and written in the traditional third-person prophetic formula (v. 7) and the "vision" proclaimed in the first person. Verse 8a states that Zechariah's vision occurred "during the night." No other time-sequence is indicated in the subsequent seven visions. Although it is possible for all of them to occur in one night, most commentators suggest that they are a succession of "experiences."

The first vision (vv. 7b-13) can be compared to focusing a telescope. One adjustment presents a large picture; additional adjustments reveal more details. Verse 8b depicts a tranquil scene. Evergreen shrubs ("myrtle trees") grow alongside streams. An equestrian stands beside his red horse, and behind him are "red, sorrel, and white horses." An exact location is not specified. The place suggests a garden like Eden, outside Jerusalem or near the entrance to heaven.

Zechariah asks the interpreting angel for an explanation (v. 9a). The angel, however, does not offer one but provides another glance at the scene (v. 9b). The central character *within the scene* identifies the horses: "These are they whom the Lord has sent to patrol the earth" (v. 10). The metaphor could point to the angels of the heavenly council (see Job 1:7; 2:2) as well as to Persian messengers, who provided a thorough communication system in the empire.

A third viewing of the scene follows. The central character ("the driver" in verse 8) becomes the "angel of the Lord" (v. 11a; see the note on "angel" above). Equestrians repeat their function: "We have patrolled the earth" and state their judgment: "see, the whole earth is tranquil and at rest" (v. 11b). Cosmic peace may be a reference to the leadership of Darius, who successfully defeated the rebellious satrapies of the empire.

A fourth glance reveals the climax of the vision. The angel of the Lord petitions the Lord of hosts to relieve the oppression of Jerusalem and Judah (v. 12). The lamentation over the situation of the returned exiles, who "felt

ingly angry with the complacent nations; whereas I was but a little angry, they added to the harm. ¹⁶Therefore, says the Lord: I will turn to Jerusalem in mercy; my house shall be built in it, says the Lord of hosts, and a measuring line shall be stretched over Jerusalem. ¹⁷Proclaim further: Thus says the Lord of hosts: My cities shall again overflow with prosperity; the Lord will again comfort Zion, and again choose Jerusalem.

2 Four Horns and Four Blacksmiths. ¹I raised my eyes and looked: there were four horns. ²Then I asked the angel who spoke with me what these were. He answered me, "These are the horns that scattered Judah and Israel and Jerusalem." ³Then the Lord showed me four blacksmiths. And I asked, "What are these coming to do?" ⁴And he said, "Here are the horns that scattered Judah, so that no man raised his head any more; but these

your anger these seventy years," is a sharp contrast to the judgment of the equestrians (v. 11). God's intervention is needed if there is to be reconstruction (compare Joel 2:14).

1:13-17 Responses. Responses to the vision function with verse 9 as an inclusion to bracket the visionary scene. Similar to the structure in Joel, a lament (v. 12) is followed by divine assurance (v. 13; see p. 17). Verse 13, however, is a *narrative* comment rather than an oracle of consolation. It serves as a transition to the oracles.

Three oracles of consolation have been appended to the vision. They respond to the lament (v. 12). Each is introduced by traditional prophetic formulas (vv. 14b, 16a, 17a). The interpreting angel exhorts Zechariah to proclaim the first and third oracles (vv. 14-15, 17).

In the first oracle (vv. 14-15), God responds. "I am deeply moved" (v. 14b) is better translated "I am exceedingly jealous" (RSV). As in Joel 2:18, the passionate zeal of God *for* Jerusalem and Zion is clear (compare Zech 8:2-3; 9:9). That zeal takes the form of anger *against* the "complacent nations" (v. 15).

The second oracle proclaims what God's zeal means for the community: "I will turn to Jerusalem in mercy" (v. 16a; compare v. 3b). The temple and the city will be restored through divine initiative (v. 16b; compare the commentary on Hag 1:2-14).

The third oracle describes the care of the Lord of hosts for "my cities" (v. 17a). Goodness, consolation, and election will again be present when God returns to Jerusalem (v. 17b). Two details are absent: the time of God's return and the outcome of the complacent nations (v. 15).

2:1-4 [1:18-21] Second vision: Four horns and four blacksmiths. This succinct vision lacks the details and oracular responses of the first vision. The visionary medium proclaims, "I raised my eyes and looked" (5:1; 6:1) and the first image, "four horns," is seen (v. 1 [1:18]). The interpreting angel is asked for assistance (v. 2a [1:19a]). The horns are identified as those who "scattered Judah and Israel and Jerusalem" (v. 2b [1:19b]).

have come to terrify them: to cast down the horns of the nations that raised their horns to scatter the land of Judah."

The New Jerusalem. ⁵Again I raised my eyes and looked: there was a man with a measuring line in his hand. ⁶"Where are you going?" I asked. "To measure Jerusalem," he answered; "to see how great is its width and how great its length."

⁷Then the angel who spoke with me advanced, and another angel came out to meet him ⁸and said to him, "Run, tell this to that young man: People will live in

Verse 3a [1:20a] states that the Lord is the agent who reveals the next image. The prophet asks about the function of the blacksmiths (v. 3b [1:20b]). The Lord responds that they "terrify" and "cast down" the "horns" who "scattered the land of Judah" (v. 4 [1:21]).

In earlier commentaries "horns" was a metaphor for world powers (Mic 4:13). The context would identify them as the enemies of northern Israel and Judah, especially Babylon. In the last decade, however, additional possibilities for interpretation have been suggested: two pairs of animal horns, four horns of the altar, horns in the ground, horn-shaped threshing tools, and horned helmets.

Similarly, "blacksmiths" in earlier commentaries was a metaphor for those who exercise judgment (see Isa 54:16-17), that is, the Persians, who reversed the fortunes of Babylon. In the last decade the term "blacksmiths" has come to identify ploughmen, artisans, constructive or destructive creators.

The thought of earlier commentaries is developed in two ways. Both highlight tasks of reconstruction. One identifies the horns as the horns belonging to animals that have roamed over the ruins of Jerusalem. When the ploughmen guide the animals back to their proper enclosures, there is space to rebuild and reconstitute the community. The other identifies the horns of the altar, which provided sanctuary for those who clung to them. After the Exile, artisans came to rebuild and purify the altar area for sanctuary and cult.

There is no specific oracle that responds to the second vision. Among the three interpretations of the vision, only the earlier one replies to the fate of the "complacent nations," which remained unaddressed in the first vision (1:15).

2:5-9 [2:1-5] Third vision: Measuring line. The third vision is introduced with the same formula as the second vision (v. 5a [v. 1a]). The new image is a man with a measuring line (vv. 5b-6 [1b-2]). This vision develops the image of the measuring device noted in the second oracle of the first vision (see 1:16).

Another new dimension is the introduction of a second angel (v. 7 [v. 3]). This angel exhorts the interpreting angel to give "that young man" (the measurer) a message about how people will live in Jerusalem. They will live "as though in open country." The Revised Standard Version translates this

Jerusalem as though in open country, because of the multitude of men and beasts in her midst. ⁹But I will be for her an encircling wall of fire, says the LORD, and I will be the glory in her midst."

¹⁰Up, up! Flee from the land of the north, says the LORD; for I scatter you to the four winds of heaven, says the LORD. ¹¹Up, escape to Zion! you who dwell in daughter Babylon. ¹²For thus said the LORD of hosts (after he had already sent me) concerning the nations that have plundered you: Whoever touches you touches the apple of my eye. ¹³See, I wave

better: "as villages without walls" (v. 8a [v. 4a]). Why "without walls"? "Because of the multitude of men and beasts in her midst" (v. 8b [v. 4b]).

A divine assurance is the climax to the vision. It parallels the oracles in the first vision (see 1:13-17). The Lord promises to be present: "an encircling wall of fire . . . the glory in her midst" (v. 9 [v. 5]).

The third vision is related to the other two visions, functioning as the third adjustment of the telescope. The first focus was cosmic; the second focus was the land of Israel; and the third is the city of Jerusalem. In addition, the third vision specifies how God "will turn to Jerusalem in mercy" (1:16a): God will offer presence and glory (2:9). These gifts suggest "prosperity" (1:17b), that is, all living things will flourish (2:8b).

The third vision is a striking illustration of the use of traditional symbols to proclaim a new reality. The "encircling wall of fire" (v. 9a [v. 5a]), which recalls God's presence as a cloud of fire during the Exodus (see Exod 13:21-22; 14:20; 40:34), is reinterpreted as the protective care of God for Jerusalem. God's initiative in rimming the city offers a perspective to human effort involved in the process of reconstruction.

The rebuilding of the temple in all its complexities is also given a new perspective. The vision of temple restoration that Ezekiel offered to the exiles as hope for the return of God's glory (see Ezek 40–48) is broadened. Zechariah's vision extends God's glory (*kabod*) to all *throughout Jerusalem.*

2:10-17 [2:6-13] Responses. The oracles consist of two sections. The first section (vv. 10-13 [vv. 6-9]) comments on the enemies of Israel mentioned in the first collection of oracles (1:15) and the second and third visions (2:1-4 [1:18-21]; compare 2:9 [2:5]). The second section continues promises of blessings for Jerusalem noted in the first collection of oracles (1:14; 16-17) and the second and third visions (2:4b [1:21b], 7-9 [3-5]). In addition to a thematic division, traditional prophetic formulas separate some of the oracles: "says the Lord" (v. 10ab [v. 6ab]; v. 14b]v. 11b]); "said the Lord of hosts" (v. 12a [v. 8a]).

There is no interpreting angel for the oracles (compare 1:13ff.). Rather, the prophet is clearly indicated as the one commissioned by God (see vv. 12a, 15b [vv. 8a, 11b]). The verses suggest that the fulfillment of God's promises will authenticate the prophet's proclamation.

my hand over them; they become plunder for their slaves. Thus you shall know that the LORD of hosts has sent me.

¹⁴Sing and rejoice, O daughter Zion! See, I am coming to dwell among you, says the LORD. ¹⁵Many nations shall join themselves to the LORD on that day, and they shall be his people, and he will dwell among you, and you shall know that the LORD of hosts has sent me to you. ¹⁶The LORD will possess Judah as his portion in the holy land, and he will again choose Jerusalem. ¹⁷Silence, all mankind, in the presence of the LORD! for he stirs forth from his holy dwelling.

3 Joshua the High Priest. ¹Then he showed me Joshua the high priest standing before the angel of the LORD, while Satan stood at his right hand to accuse him. ²And the angel of the LORD said to Satan, "May the LORD rebuke you, Satan; may the LORD who has chosen Jerusa-

The first section of oracles contains imperatives for the exiles and warnings for those who conquered them. There is a parallel construction for verses 10 and 11. Those who are living in "the land of the north" (v. 10a [v. 6a]; see Jer 3:18; 16:15; 23:8; 31:8) are identical with the ones "who dwell in daughter Babylon" (v. 11b [v. 7b]).

The exiles are exhorted to "flee" and "escape to Zion" before God "scatters" the inhabitants of Babylon "to the four winds of heaven" (vv. 10-11a [vv. 6-7a]). In these verses the identification of Babylon is probably more extensive than the geographical region designated as exilic territory. It includes all oppressors of Israel.

An ironic punishment is pronounced for the nations that plundered Israel (v. 12a [v. 8a]): "they become plunder for their slaves" (v. 13a [v. 9a]). Why such harsh treatment? "Whoever touches you touches the apple of my eye" (v. 12b [v. 8b]). The metaphor indicates "pupil" or "gate" of the eye, that is, a treasured part or relationship.

The second section, like the third vision (see vv. 8-9 [vv. 4-5]), presents new revelation in traditional terms. Let those in Jerusalem rejoice (see Zeph 3:14-15; Zech 9:9; Pss 9:14; 48:11). The Lord is coming to dwell with the temple-community (v. 14 [v. 10]). The Hebrew of the verse indicates the language of manifestation and abiding presence.

The Lord's dwelling is mentioned in the next verse (v. 15 [v. 11]) with unexpected proclamations. "On that day," referring to the day of the Lord (see the commentary on Joel 2:18–4:21 [2:18–3:21]), the "many nations" shall "join themselves to the Lord . . . and they shall be his people." How the nations will be joined or how Israel and the nations shall become a "people" is not indicated. The concept of the Lord's dwelling among the nations and Israel is remarkable, especially when compared with Zechariah's contemporary Haggai. The latter limited the nations' contributions to their treasures for the temple (see the commentary on Hag 2:7-9).

Covenant language ("choose") is used to indicate the Lord's relationship to Judah and Jerusalem (v. 16 [11]). The designation of Judah as "holy land"

lem rebuke you! Is not this man a brand snatched from the fire?"

³Now Joshua was standing before the angel, clad in filthy garments. ⁴He spoke and said to those who were standing before him, "Take off his filthy garments, and clothe him in festal garments." ⁵He also said, "Put a clean miter on his head." And they put a clean miter on his head and clothed him with the garments. Then the angel of the LORD, standing, said, "See, I have taken away your guilt."

appears only here. Everything will be holy because of the Lord's dwelling among the people.

The responses conclude with a fragment of liturgical directive: "Silence . . . in the presence of the Lord!" (v. 17a [v. 13a]; compare Hab 2:20; Zeph 1:7).

3:1-5 Fourth vision: Joshua the high priest. Chapter 3 is presented without any rearrangement of the verses (see p. 59). The vision differs from the first three visions in form. There is no introductory statement, question about interpretation, or explanation by the angel. Some commentators suggest that the unusual form indicates a later vision that was added to an original seven visions.

Verse 1 is an introduction to the vision. The "he" probably refers to the interpreting angel who accompanied the prophet during the first three visions (v. 1a; see 1:9, 14; 2:2, 7 [1:19; 2:3]). Three characters appear in the vision of the heavenly council (v. 1b):

a) "Joshua the high priest" appears for the first time (see pp. 46–47).

b) "The angel of the Lord" who appeared in the first three visions convenes and authorizes the proceedings of the heavenly council (see vv. 2, 4-5).

c) "Satan" is a transliteration of the Hebrew word that means "adversary." It is not a personal name in the Hebrew Bible; rather, it designates a role, that is, accuser (see Job 1:6-12; 2:1-7; Ps 109:6; Rev 12:10).

Verse 2 ironically reverses the roles of Satan and Joshua. Whatever accusations the adversary had spoken against Joshua are abrogated by the double rebukes of the "Lord who has chosen Jerusalem" (see 1:17b; 2:16 [2:12]; compare Hag 2:23). Verse 2 concludes with a rhetorical question: "Is not this man a brand snatched from the fire?" (see Amos 4:11). As Joshua represents the entire community in verse 1, here their communal deliverance from exile is suggested (v. 2b).

The position of Joshua before the angel of the Lord (v. 3a) repeats verse 1a. The "filthy garments" that Joshua wears (v. 3b) are associated with the fire imagery of the Exile experience (v. 2b). The garments could symbolize mourning (see Jer 41:4-5) or the guilt associated with living in Babylon.

The authoritative angel of the Lord directs the angels of the council to reclothe Joshua (vv. 4-5). "Festal garments" and a "clean miter" replace the filthy garments. According to some commentators, the ritual dressing indi-

⁶The angel of the LORD then gave Joshua this assurance: ⁷"Thus says the LORD of hosts: If you walk in my ways and heed my charge, you shall judge my house and keep my courts, and I will give you access among these standing here. ⁸Listen, O Joshua, high priest! You and your associates who sit before you are men of good omen. Yes, I will bring my servant the Shoot. ⁹Look at the stone that

cates garb of the high priest (see Lev 8:1-9). Others propose a figurative context of acceptance in the court (see Isa 62:3; Job 29:14).

The ritual activity symbolizes the judgment of the angel: "See, I have taken away your guilt" (v. 5b). "Guilt" suggests the association of Joshua with the land of Babylon as well as the transgressions of the temple-community, of which he is the religious leader (see Exod 28:36-38; Num 18:1). To function as high priest, the ritual activity was necessary. The temple ritual for purification is not available.

3:6-10 Responses. A challenge and two oracles of assurance interpret the fourth vision. Each is prefaced by a traditional prophetic formula: "says the Lord of hosts" (vv. 7a, 9b, 10a). Each proclamation is directed to Joshua the high priest by the authoritative angel (v. 6).

The challenge is made in verse 7a: "If you walk in my ways and heed my charge . . . ." The first condition refers to moral integrity (see Deut 8:6), while the second is more ambiguous. The Hebrew term suggests a general obligation or prohibition (see Gen 26:5; Lev 18:30), or a duty (Isa 21:8). It also signifies ritual activity (see Num 3). In this context the faithful cultic service of God is apt.

Acceptance of the challenge results in two areas of responsibility (and blessing) in verse 7b. Each one reflects the situation of a *preexilic monarch.* "Judge my house" indicates judicial functions (see Deut 17:8-13), while "keep my courts" refers to decisions about cultic activity. Both responsibilities are carried out at the temple. The judicial functions *there* are new for a high priest (compare Ezek 44:10-31). "Access among these standing here" describes Joshua's approach to the members of the heavenly council.

The second oracle is an unconditional blessing for Joshua and his associates (v. 8). The identity of the group is unclear. Some commentators suggest additional priests or persons of prominence in the temple-community (see Ezra 2; Neh 7). In what sense are they a "good omen"? They are considered signs of God's blessing (v. 8b; 6:12-13). The "branch" imagery was a traditional one for a just ruler (see Jer 23:5; Isa 11:1). The appearance of a monarch like David is part of the expectation of restoration of the temple-community. Haggai, Zechariah's contemporary, had proclaimed that possibility for Zerubbabel (see Hag 2:23). Verses 7 and 8 suggest some type of shared rule. The high priest (and other priests) functions in the temple, while a Davidic heir functions on the throne.

I have placed before Joshua, one stone with seven facets. I will engrave its inscription, says the LORD of hosts, and I will take away the guilt of the land in one day. ¹⁰On that day, says the LORD of hosts, you will invite one another under your vines and fig trees."

4 ⁴Then I said to the angel who spoke with me, "What are these things, my lord?" ⁵And the angel who spoke with me replied, "Do you not know what these things are?" "No, my lord," I answered. ⁶Then he said to me, "This is the LORD's message to Zerubbabel: Not by an army,

Verse 9a continues the second oracle with another image: "one stone with seven facets." Attention returns to Joshua (see v. 7) as the one before whom the stone is placed. The stone might be a person; a real stone for temple reconstruction; a stone for ritual purposes; a stone belonging to the garb of high priest.

Verse 9b provides additional details about the stone, which clarify its identity. It probably is the engraved stone that adorned the high priest's turban (see Exod 28:36-38). Its inscription, "Sacred to the Lord" (Exod 28:36), suggests cleansing from guilt (see Exod 28:38).

Something new is revealed. Aaron (and his successors) *"bears* whatever guilt the Israelites may incur" (Exod 28:38a). The Lord of hosts *removes* the "guilt of the land in one day" (v. 9b). This completes the process that the angel of the Lord started by removing Joshua's guilt (v. 5). Now God's initiative cleanses the land.

Verse 10 completes the challenge and oracles of assurance. "On that day" identifies a future possibility wherein the community will be at home and extend hospitality, (see 1 Kgs 5:25 [4:25]; Mic 4:4).

4:1-6a, 10b-14 Fifth vision: Lampstand. There is some rearrangement of verses in chapter 4. Note the difference between the New American Bible text above and the arrangement of the commentary (see p. 59).

The introductory statement of the fifth vision presents the interpreting angel, who stirs up the prophet (v. 1; compare Joel 4:9 [3:9]). Verse 1 may be a literary device to unify the material between the first vision "at night" (see 1:8) and the present one.

Verse 2a is a departure from the first four visions, where the prophet immediately reports what he sees. This time the interpreting angel asks the question (compare 5:1-4). Zechariah responds with a detailed description of a gold lampstand (vv. 2b-3).

The prophet questions the angel about "these things" (v. 4). The angel responds with another question, implying that the image ought to be clear (v. 5a). After the prophet admits he does not know (v. 5b), the angel explains the scene by first interpreting the lamp (vv. 6a, 10b). The seven "facets" (lights) on the lampstand are "the eyes of the Lord that range over the whole earth."

nor by might, but by my spirit, says the Lord of hosts. [7]What are you, O great mountain? Before Zerubbabel you are but a plain. He shall bring out the capstone amid exclamations of 'Hail, Hail' to it."

[8]This word of the Lord then came to me: [9]The hands of Zerubbabel have laid the foundations of this house, and his hands shall finish it; then you shall know that the Lord of hosts has sent me to you.

The prophet inquires again about the "two olive trees at each side of the lampstand" (v. 11). Another question follows: "What are the two olive tufts which freely pour out fresh oil through the two golden channels?" (v. 12). Again, the interpreting angel is surprised that the prophet does not recognize the image (v. 13). When the prophet admits that he does not know (v. 13), the angel explains (v. 14).

How may the major components of the vision be interpreted? A description of the lampstand explains the basic structure of the vision. Within the last century archeological discoveries have classified a number of clay lamps and lampstands conforming to a particular shape. A lampstand is at the base. Resting on the stand is a bowl for oil. On the rim of the bowl are indentations for wicks (usually approximately seven). When the wicks are ignited, they burn because they are draped over the oil.

Although the term for the lampstand is *menorah,* it does not match the description of the seven-branched candelabrum used in ritual contexts (see Exod 25:33). What is unusual in the description of the lampstand in the vision is not its shape but its composition of gold.

What does the lampstand symbolize? The lampstand and lights represent the presence of God, who looks kindly upon all of creation (see 2 Chr 16:9; compare Ezra 5:5). The lampstand and lights parallel and develop two images of earlier visions: the equestrians who patrol the earth (1:10-11) and the encircling wall of fire (2:9).

The olive trees (vv. 3, 11) and the olive tufts (v. 12) are clearly interpreted by the angel as the "two anointed who stand by the Lord of the whole earth" (v. 14). Who are the "anointed"? They are Zerubbabel and Joshua, equal in dignity and importance. Their proposed rule is unexpected because only a monarch like David was anticipated. Nonetheless, for the temple-community there are two who will govern. After Zerubbabel's death the office of high priest grew in prominence (see pp. 10–11).

Many commentators considered Zerubbabel and Joshua as messiah figures because of the "anointed" terminology. The Hebrew phrase translates "sons of oil." In addition, the oil is of the type used for harvest festivals, not for an anointing ceremony. As high priest, Joshua had already been anointed. The two rulers function, however, in a revolutionary role. Although verse 12 is difficult to translate, the imagery suggests that Zerubbabel and Joshua are close to God, who needs their oil for the agency of compassionate presence

¹⁰For even they who were scornful on that day of small beginnings shall rejoice to see the select stone in the hands of Zerubbabel. These seven facets are the eyes of the LORD that range over the whole earth.

The Lampstand. ¹Then the angel who spoke with me returned and awakened me, like a man awakened from his sleep. ²"What do you see?" he asked me. "I see a lampstand all of gold, with a bowl at the top," I replied; "on it are seven lamps with their tubes, ³and beside it are two olive trees, one on the right and the other on the left." ¹¹I then asked him, "What

("seven facets") for the community. They, in turn, require God's support for leadership. The interdependency is new.

4:6b-10a Collection of responses. If the verses were not rearranged, they would appear between the description of the lampstand and its interpretation. The verses are a poetic insertion consisting of two oracles. Both are introduced by traditional prophetic formulas: "This is the Lord's message" (v. 6b); "This word of the Lord then came to me" (v. 8; see 6:9; 7:4; 8:1, 18). The oracles describe Zerubbabel's leadership in restoring the temple, as an earlier visionary ritual had described Joshua's preparation for the office of high priest (3:1-10).

The first oracle (vv. 6b-7) describes how the work of temple restoration will be accomplished. Neither an "army" (compare 1 Kgs 5:20) nor "might" (see Neh 4:10) is adequate to the task. Divine activity will complete the work (v. 6b).

Since God's spirit is with Zerubbabel, he is the leader in the temple reconstruction. First, Zerubbabel is compared metaphorically to a mountain of obstacles and emerges as the greater one (v. 7a; see Isa 40:4; 41:15). Second, he will bear the "capstone" amid exclamations of the community.

Commentators debate the identity of the capstone. Is it the foundation stone or the final stone on the pinnacle of the temple? Some see the oracles (vv. 6b-10a) and the visionary ritual of Joshua (3:1-10) in the wider context of Mesopotamian services for rededication of the temple. The capstone signifies continuity. It is a stone taken from the earlier temple and positioned in the new one to assure cultic continuity. The "select stone" (v. 10a) refers to another type of ritual—placing an engraved tin tablet into the edifice of the new temple.

Others propose that the capstone is the final piece of the new temple. It is the "select stone" (v. 10a) placed by the hands of Zerubbabel, the civic governor of the temple-community. The Hebrew terms used to describe the stone allow both interpretations. In general, Zechariah was convinced that Zerubbabel's leadership was necessary for the project (see 6:12-13).

The second oracle (vv. 9-10a) connects the activity of Zerubbabel with the credibility of the prophet. The Lord's proclamation assures Zechariah that Zerubbabel, who began the foundation, will finish it (v. 9a). The com-

are these two olive trees at each side of the lampstand?" [12]And again I asked, "What are the two olive tufts which freely pour out fresh oil through the two golden channels?" [13]"Do you not know what these are?" he said to me. "No, my lord," I answered him. [14]He said, "These are the two anointed who stand by the LORD of the whole earth."

5 The Flying Scroll.
[1]Then I raised my eyes again and saw a scroll flying. [2]"What do you see?" he asked me. I answered, "I see a scroll flying; it is twenty cubits long and ten cubits wide." [3]Then he said to me: "This is the curse which is to go forth over the whole earth; in accordance with it shall every thief be swept away, and in accordance with it shall ev-

pletion of the temple will be a sign to the community that Zechariah's proclamations are validated (v. 9b; compare 2:9, 11; 6:15).

Verse 10a describes the general attitude of the temple-community toward the task of reconstruction (compare Hag 2:3-5; Ezra 3:12). Even these scoffers "shall rejoice to see the select stone in the hands of Zerubbabel." The four references to Zerubbabel's hands (4:7 [implicit]; 9 [twice]; 10a) may refer to his royal function in the cultic ceremonies of temple restoration. In ancient Near East traditions the king often assisted in temple reconstruction either actually or symbolically.

5:1-4 Sixth vision: Flying scroll. The spatial quality and movement of the vision parallel the seventh vision: the flying bushel (5:5-11). Both visions are directed to the temple-community. What is necessary to cleanse the community for renewed relationship with God? The theme of renewal, addressed to Joshua with regard to cult (3:1-10) and to Zerubbabel with regard to temple reconstruction (4:6b-10a), has specific implications for the community as well.

Verse 1 is the introductory statement and description of the flying scroll. It repeats the literary form of the second and third visions (see 2:1 [1:18]; 2:5 [2:1]). The short formula will be repeated in the eighth vision (see 6:1).

The question of the interpreting angel (v. 2a) appears redundant, since the prophet had already announced his vision (v. 1). The vision is described with additional detail (v. 2b). While a scroll would be a familiar sight (see Jer 36:1-8) and symbol (see Ezek 2:9-10; 3:1-3), the proportions are unusual. A scroll is much longer than it is wide. In addition, although no one is holding the scroll, it is unrolled and flying in the air!

The dimensions of the scroll match the area of Solomon's temple porch (see 1 Kgs 6:3) and are similar to those of the desert sanctuary, which is half the size (see Exod 26:15-28). However, there is no apparent connection between the flying scroll and either area.

The interpreting angel identifies the scroll as a "curse . . . over the whole earth"; it will sweep away "every thief" and expel "every perjurer" (v. 3). The curse refers to consequences for covenant abrogations that were added to the ceremony by oaths (see Deut 28:15ff.; compare Gen 26:28; Ezek 17:13).

ery perjurer be expelled from here. [4]I will send it forth, says the LORD of hosts, and it shall come into the house of the thief, or into the house of him who perjures himself with my name; it shall lodge within his house, consuming it, timber and stones."

The Flying Bushel. [5]Then the angel who spoke with me came forward and said to me, "Raise your eyes and see what this is that comes forth." [6]"What is it?" I asked. And he answered, "This is a bushel container coming. This is their guilt in all the land." [7]Then a leaden cover was lifted, and there was a woman sitting inside the bushel. [8]"This is Wickedness," he said; and he thrust her inside the bushel, pushing the leaden cover into the

The thought in verses 3-4 is a fusion of the covenant stipulations and the Decalogue prescriptions. Specifically, the thief represents the laws regarding human conduct (see Exod 20:15-16), and the perjurer represents attitudes toward God (see Exod 20:7).

Verse 4 is a divine oracle that interprets the vision. It tells of the consequences for thief and perjurer. Their houses and inhabitants will be consumed by the curse that God sends forth (compare Ps 147:15; Isa 55:11).

What is the particular situation in the community that draws attention to thievery and perjury? The perpetrators of these crimes are forbidden to enter the temple (see Ps 24:4). Thievery was a particular problem for the temple-community, especially the usurpation of land tracts by those who remained in Judah during the Babylonian Captivity (see p. 10). Litigation occurred. The charge of perjury is probably related to these occasions.

The curse of the flying scroll may also represent the continuity of judgment and values. Even though the community will be administered by a new model of leadership (Joshua and Zerubbabel), the standards will remain the same as before (compare the commentary on 4:6b-10a). Another factor of continuity is the phrase "the whole earth" (v. 3a). Within both Judah and the Diaspora the same obligations for all Jews will be in force.

5:5-11 Seventh vision: Flying bushel. The vision is inaugurated by a command of the interpreting angel to look up and identify the new symbol (v. 5). The familiar question pattern follows (v. 6a), with the angel's response (v. 6b). The vision reveals another character: "a woman sitting inside the bushel" is "Wickedness," whom the angel thrusts inside, "pushing the leaden cover into the opening" (vv. 7-8).

Next the prophet sees additional characters. Two women with ruffled wings like a stork's lift the bushel into the air (v. 9). The prophet seeks assistance from the angel, who explains the women's action. They are taking the bushel to Shinar, where they will deposit it in the temple when the building is completed (vv. 10-11).

The bushel container and the woman are central to the vision. Their relationship is the key to interpretation. The bushel container functions as the

opening. ⁹Then I raised my eyes and saw two women coming forth with a wind ruffling their wings, for they had wings like the wings of a stork. As they lifted up the bushel into the air, ¹⁰I said to the angel who spoke with me, "Where are they taking the bushel?" ¹¹He replied, "To build a temple for it in the land of Shinar; when the temple is ready, they will deposit it there in its place."

6 **Four Chariots.** ¹Again I raised my eyes and saw four chariots coming

"setting" for both parts of the vision. The term in Hebrew means "container" (see Ruth 2:17) and a "measure" or standardized weight (see Amos 8:5; Ezek 45:10). The prophet's question, "What is it?" refers to content as well as measure.

The question of content is immediately clarified by the angel: "their guilt in all the land" (v. 7b). What is the source of guilt? The woman named Wickedness is the symbol of evil surrounded by guilt (v. 8). Like the genie in the bottle and unlike Pandora and her box, Wickedness and guilt can be controlled by the leaden cover that the angel thrusts into the opening of the container.

Many speculate about why the woman personifies wickedness. Some refer to the feminine gender of the Hebrew word for "wickedness." Others associate it with Israel's sin, which is often described by use of the metaphor of harlotry (see Jer 3:8; Hos 1:2; Ezek 16). A few point to the garden event (Gen 3) as the origin of the personification.

Two figures, half-animal (stork wings) and half-human (women), appear as *deae ex machina* to remove the bushel basket. Stork wings suggest flying animals (see Jer 8:7) and unclean animals (see Lev 11:9; Deut 14:18). Soaring in the wind, they carry the container to Shinar, an ancient name for the land of Babylon (see Gen 10:10; 11:2; Dan 1:2; Rev 14:8). There Wickedness and guilt will have a temple in which to reside.

The image of removing evil and guilt is parallel to the image of Joshua's "filthy garments" (3:3). God initiates the removal of extensive evil ("in all the land") of the community and the impurity of the high priest through agents—two women and the angel (3:5). God is not contaminated by impurity or evil.

The bushel container and the woman are considered non-standards for the temple-community that has returned to restore relationship with God. Covenant obligations (5:1-4) and the removal of evil and guilt are dimensions of reconstruction.

6:1-8 Eighth vision: Four chariots. The final vision forms an inclusion with the first vision (1:7-12). The first verse (1:7) and the last verse (8:8) indicate visionary experience. Details of place (glen, mountain pass) and time (night, sunrise) are different. Important images, however, parallel one another: horses, colors, patrolling functions.

out from between two mountains; and the mountains were of bronze. ²The first chariot had red horses, the second chariot black horses, ³the third chariot white horses, and the fourth chariot spotted horses—all of them strong horses. ⁴I asked the angel who spoke with me, "What are these, my lord?" ⁵The angel said to me in reply, "These are the four winds of the heavens, which are coming forth after being reviewed by the LORD of all the earth." ⁶The chariot with the black horses was turning toward the land of the north, the red and the white horses went after them, and the spotted ones went toward the land of the south. ⁷As these strong horses emerged, eager to set about patrolling the earth, he said, "Go, patrol the earth!" Then, as they patrolled the earth, ⁸he called out to me and said, "See, they that go forth to the land of the north will make my spirit rest in the land of the north."

The Coronation. ⁹This word of the LORD then came to me: ¹⁰Take from the returned captives Heldai, Tobijah, Jedaiah; and go the same day to the house of Josiah, son of Zephaniah (these had

Verse 1 is a short introductory statement with an initial description of the vision; details appear in verses 2-3. Four chariots emerge between two "bronze mountains" (v. 1). Each chariot is numbered and described by a colored horse (red, black, white, spotted) that pulls it. All the horses are "strong" (vv. 2-3).

The question of the prophet (v. 4) is readily answered by the interpreting angel (v. 5). The chariots turn in different directions (v. 6). While anticipating their patrolling function, the "strong horses" are commanded directly by God (vv. 6b-7a). While they are patrolling the earth, God issues a second command to the prophet (v. 8).

The final vision reveals personified "winds" patrolling the earth for the Lord, whose abode is protected by two bronze mountains. The chariots are primary, while the number and color of the horses are secondary details (vv. 2-3). They may resemble military forces (see 2 Kgs 23:11; Ps 104:4) that are eager to facilitate conditions so that the Lord's spirit may "rest in the land of the north" (v. 8b).

The first and eighth visions function as opening and closing scenes of the night visions. In the first vision toward nightfall, the report of the equestrians patrolling the earth indicates that "the whole earth is tranquil and at rest" (1:11). Nonetheless, there is a plea for mercy on behalf of the temple-community, which does not experience that "rest" (1:12). The Lord is moved to compassion for the community but is "exceedingly angry with the complacent nations" (1:16).

The intervening visions present the plight of the community, especially the importance of dual leadership, temple restoration, and purgation. In contrast, the situation of the oppressors of Israel is included briefly (see 2:1-4, 12-13). The phrase "the whole earth" and movement patterns characterize the process of the visions.

come from Babylon). ¹¹Silver and gold you shall take, and make a crown; place it on the head of [Joshua, son of Jehozadak, the high priest] Zerubbabel. ¹²And say to him: Thus says the LORD of hosts: Here is a man whose name is Shoot, and where he is he shall sprout, and he shall build the temple of the LORD. ¹³Yes, he shall build the temple of the LORD, and taking up the royal insignia, he shall sit

In the eighth vision there is tranquility because God's spirit is at rest "in the land of the north." The downfall of the oppressors as well as the return of the exiles to Jerusalem signals a new reality. Exact chronology is not a concern in any of the visionary narratives or oracular responses.

6:9-15 Responses and a crown. The structure of the final section of the eighth vision consists of two oracles. The first oracle (vv. 9-11, 14-15) frames the second oracle (vv. 12-13). The first oracle is a private proclamation to the prophet: "This word of the Lord came to me" (v. 9), while the second oracle is a public proclamation: "And say to him: 'Thus says the Lord of hosts' " (v. 12a). Both oracles respond to the visions whose reality will occur when the temple is completed. The oracles in their final, edited form, however, focus on an indefinite future.

After the oracular introduction (v. 9) the prophet is commanded by God to take something from the "returned captives Heldai, Tobijah, Jedaiah" (v. 10a). What the returnees possess becomes clear in verse 11: "silver and gold." The names are not found in Jewish tradition. Their orthodox position in returning to Jerusalem is indicated by their *theophoric* names, that is, the consonants for Yahweh appear in their names. They also represent others in the Diaspora who contribute materials for temple restoration.

The returnees are commanded to go immediately to the "house of Josiah, son of Zephaniah (these had come from Babylon)" (v. 10b). There may be continuity between the two groups of returned exiles if Josiah had been taken into exile. On the other hand, if he had remained in Judah, there would be continuity in the two groups who now lived on the land restoring the temple.

The silver and gold brought back from exile will be fashioned into a "crown" (v. 11a). Other ancient texts read "crowns." Arguments based on subsequent verses are persuasive for both the singular and plural forms of the noun. The discussion about "crown" is the beginning of many difficult textual decisions in the section.

Who will wear the crown? The New American Bible states: "place it on the head of [Joshua, son of Jehozadak, the high priest] Zerubbabel" (v. 11b). The Revised Standard Version and the New English Bible, however, delete the reference to Zerubbabel and the brackets around the Joshua description. Again, there are persuasive arguments for either Joshua or Zerubbabel and the crown.

as ruler upon his throne. The priest shall be at his right hand, and between the two of them there shall be friendly understanding. [14]The crown itself shall be a memorial offering in the temple of the LORD in favor of Heldai, Tobijah, Jedaiah, and the son of Zephaniah. [15]And they who are from afar shall come and build the temple of the LORD, and you shall know that the LORD of hosts has sent me to you. And if you heed carefully the voice of the LORD your God. . . .

Those favoring Joshua note that the fate of Zerubbabel is unclear in the tradition. The final editor probably inserted Joshua's name to clarify what happened historically, that is, the high priest became the source of authority for the temple-community (see p. 10).

Commentators who propose Zerubbabel's name refer to his function as the temple-builder (see 4:9; compare 4:12). He would be the logical one to be crowned in a royal ceremony, since the installation as high priest would be a separate ceremony. Others argue that the coronation had to be symbolic due to the position of the temple-community of Judah within the Persian empire.

One scholar noted that Zerubbabel's role was diminished in the lampstand vision by its position in the middle of the vision. Now, Joshua's role is similarly diminished by its position in the middle of the final oracles.

Finally, since a two-person rule had been a possibility suggested before in visionary material (see 4:1-5, 10b-14), *two* crowns may be apt for Zerubbabel and Joshua.

A public oracle of the Lord follows the description of the crown (vv. 12-13). Its focus is temple reconstruction (see 4:6-10a), in particular an individual who has an important role in the project. The person is identified as "Shoot," a name used to describe a future Davidic figure (see the commentary on 3:8). Zerubbabel is the logical referent drawn from 3:8 as well as from the additional detail at the end of the verse: "he shall build the temple" (v. 12b).

The choice of Zerubbabel is strengthened by the details of verse 13. The first part repeats the function of temple-builder and adds the royal function of ruling from the throne (v. 13a). The priest mentioned in the second part of the verse is probably Joshua. Both reign from the throne area, yet Joshua appears to claim more status. "Friendly understanding" describes their new model of leadership for the temple-community (v. 13b).

The next two verses are the conclusion of the first oracle (vv. 9-11, 14-15). The symbolic function of the crown (see the commentary on v. 11b) is described (v. 14). While memorial offerings on behalf of the community were known (see Exod 30:16), the crown will immortalize several individuals.

A comparison of the names in verses 14 and 10 indicates that two of the four names are different: Heldai and Helem (Hebrew text); Josiah and Hen

7 True Fasting. ¹In the fourth year of Darius the king [the word of the LORD came to Zechariah], on the fourth day of Chislev, the ninth month, ²Bethel-sarezer sent Regemmelech and his men to implore favor of the LORD ³and to ask the priests of the house of the LORD of hosts, and the prophets, "Must I mourn and abstain in

(Hebrew text). In addition, the function of Joshua changes from one whose house served as a meeting place (v. 10b) to one who will be immortalized with the other three (v. 14b). Some commentators suggest that Helem and Hen are nicknames for Heldai and Josiah.

Verse 15 reiterates themes mentioned in the visions and response oracles. First, there is an acknowledgment of assistance for temple reconstruction from those "who are from afar." Not only will they send materials (see v. 11), but they will actively engage in the process (v. 15a).

Second, the cooperation in rebuilding will be another sign of the prophet's authentication from God (v. 15b). The other signs described a new relationship between the temple-community and God (see the commentary on 2:13 [2:9]) as well as leadership for the temple reconstruction (see the commentary on 4:9b).

Third, the last part of the verse, which is incomplete, presents a challenge that was neglected by ancestors before the Exile. It suggests that obedience to the Lord is adhering to the visions and oracles of Zechariah. The challenge offers the community a new beginning and an opportunity for returning to God as God desires to return to the community. The final words of First Zechariah, then, form an inclusion with the first divine oracle (see 1:3ff.).

PART THREE: ORACLES ABOUT FASTING AND THE FUTURE

Zech 7:1–8:23

Part Three consists of the final two chapters of First Zechariah. It is a collection of oracles arranged from various contexts to form a coherent message. The sections present hortatory material that could be developed in greater detail for preaching occasions. The tone of the oracles is an interweaving of encouragement and warning, with constant reference to past experience as a model for present and future activity. The basic structure of chapter 7 is a question-and-answer format, while chapter 8 is a series of ten proclamations. It is impossible to separate the prophet's oracles from the elaboration of the editor.

7:1-3 Question about fasting. The superscription combines a traditional prophetic formula and a precise chronology (v. 1). It is one year after the visions and two years after the beginning of temple restoration, that is, November-December 518 B.C.E. The chronology also indicates the ninth

the fifth month as I have been doing these many years?" ⁴Thereupon this word of the LORD of hosts came to me: ⁵Say to all the people of the land and to the priests: When you fasted and mourned in the fifth and in the seventh month these seventy years, was it really for me that you fasted? ⁶And when you were eating and drinking, was it not for yourselves that you ate, and for yourselves that you drank? ⁷Were not these the words which the LORD spoke through the former

month of the year (Chislev). The notation of month occurs in one other super-scription (1:7). The mention of Darius as king occurs here and in Hag 1:1 (see the commentary on Hag 1:1).

Verse 2 introduces individuals who are new to the temple at Jerusalem. Scholarly discussion suggests that Bethelsarezer was a Jewish official in Babylon who acted on behalf of his community. He sent Regemmelech and his retinue to Jerusalem with a request. The phrase "implore the favor of the Lord" describes a situation needing immediate attention (see Exod 32:11). Note that the phrase is structurally parallel to "ask the priests of the house of the Lord of hosts, and the prophets" (v. 3a).

The "priests of the house of the Lord" and the "prophets" (v. 3a) describe those who functioned with authority in the temple-community after the Exile (compare Mic 3:11). Since the verse implies that temple restoration had been completed, it may be an editorial remark. Nonetheless, the cooperation of both groups is needed to address the community's plight both in Babylon and Jerusalem. Their response would probably affect Jews throughout the Diaspora as well. Ironically, the text indicates only the response of the prophet.

The question before the authorities concerns ritual activities of mourning and abstaining (v. 3b). The temple had been destroyed in the fifth month (2 Kgs 25:8-9). Consequently, rituals were observed to commemorate that event. Ought any community observe them now that reconstruction on the temple was in progress? According to several commentators, a deeper question is implied. Has the promise of the prophets been fulfilled? Are we living in a new age following upon the restoration of the temple? If so, mourning is transformed by rejoicing.

7:4-7 Responses. The replies are two oracles consisting of rhetorical questions from God and one from Zechariah. The divine-oracle formula is found in verse 4, and verse 5a states that "all the people of the land" (compare Hag 2:4), including the priests, will be the addressees of the proclamation. In verse 5b another time for ritual mourning commemorates the assassination of Gedaliah, the Jewish governor of Jerusalem, who had been appointed by Babylon (2 Kgs 25:22-26; see p. 8).

The first question focuses on intentions for fasting and mourning (v. 5b). The second question follows immediately. Wasn't the opposite situation of

prophets, when Jerusalem and the surrounding cities were inhabited and at peace, when the Negeb and the foothills were inhabited? [8][This word of the LORD came to Zechariah: [9]Thus says the LORD of hosts:] Render true judgment, and show kindness and compassion toward each other. [10]Do not oppress the widow or the orphan, the alien or the poor; do not plot evil against one another in your hearts. [11]But they refused to listen; they stubbornly turned their backs and stopped their ears so as not to hear. [12]And they made their hearts diamondhard so as not to hear the teaching and the message that the LORD of hosts had sent by his spirit through the former prophets. [13]Then the LORD of hosts in his great anger

eating and drinking also "for yourselves"? (v. 6). Self-centeredness is the attitude challenged in both situations (compare Hag 1:4-8, 10; Isa 58:3-7, 13).

Zechariah's rhetorical question is a comment on the Lord's question (v. 7). He draws attention to the tradition of the community before the Exile. The "former prophets" had spoken God's word when Judah was populated and at peace (v. 7b). Their collective proclamation vindicates his message, too. Zechariah had spoken about a meager population in Judah after the Exile (see 2:10 [2:8]; compare 2:8 [2:4]). He may be suggesting that fasting before and after the Exile is problematic; its focus is on the individual, not God.

7:8-14 Another collection of responses. These verses can be divided according to topic. Verses 8-10 interrupt the response about fasting (vv. 4-7). They present a summary of ethical teaching promulgated by the prophets before the Exile. Verses 11-14 return to the response about fasting.

Verses 8-9a introduce a divine oracle with a traditional prophetic formula. The oracle (vv. 9b-10) states the genuine nature of fasting proclaimed in earlier tradition. The first part is a general maxim for social conduct: be honest in judgment; be compassionate toward one another (v. 9b; see Jer 7:5). The maxim is reinforced by specific prohibitions (v. 10; see Jer 7:6; compare 1:4b).

Verses 11-14 provide a picture of the community before the Exile (compare 1:3b-6) as a model for reflection. The admonitory style is similar to the Chronicler's (see 2 Chr 30:6-9; Neh 9:25-31). The instruction issues warnings and provides hope. The section reinforces Zechariah's and the editor's claim to authority.

Earlier communities had refused to listen to the Lord's imperative about true fasting (v. 11a). Metaphors of body language dramatize their stubbornness (vv. 11b-12a). What were they resisting? "The teaching and the message that the Lord of hosts had sent by his spirit through the former prophets" (v. 12b). No one but the prophets was entrusted with God's teaching and message (compare 1:4). A closer relationship between God and the prophets is indicated by the phrase "his spirit." Since the prophets shared in God's spirit, to reject them is virtually to reject God.

said that, as they had not listened when he called, so he would not listen when they called, ¹⁴but would scatter them with a whirlwind among all the nations that they did not know. Thus the land was left desolate after them with no one traveling to and fro; they made the pleasant land into a desert.

8 In the Days of the Messiah. ¹This word of the LORD of hosts came: Thus says the LORD of hosts:

²I am intensely jealous for Zion,
  stirred to jealous wrath for her.

³   Thus says the LORD:
I will return to Zion,
  and I will dwell within Jerusalem;
Jerusalem shall be called the faithful city,
  and the mountain of the LORD of hosts,
  the holy mountain.

⁴Thus says the LORD of hosts: Old men and old women, each with staff in hand because of old age, shall again sit in the streets of Jerusalem. ⁵The city shall be filled with boys and girls playing in her

God's response to the community's stubbornness was reciprocal: "he would not listen when they called" (v. 13). The concluding verse extends the consequences of the preexilic community through the Exile and the restoration attempts of the current community. God acted by scattering the community "among all the nations that they did not know" (v. 14a). The land, too, suffered: it became desolate (v. 14b).

8:1-8 Blessings for Jerusalem. Two prophetic formulas introduce the first oracle (vv. 2-3). The omission of "to me" indicates that Zechariah is repeating what he had heard before (v. 1). God's "intense jealousy" of, and "wrath" toward, Zion indicates passion and concern for the returned exiles (v. 2). The proclamation functioned initially as a response to the first vision (see 1:14). Verse 2 also initiates promises of blessings (8:2-23) following the oracles of warnings (7:4-17).

Verse 3 states how God will respond to the community. Again the language parallels the response after the first vision (see 1:16). In both sections God "will return to Zion . . . and . . . will dwell within Jerusalem" (v. 3a). God's dwelling recalls how the people and God lived in tents (see Exod 25:8; 29:46). However, there is a new revelation here. God's *presence* initiates a new name for Jerusalem: "faithful" and "holy mountain" (v. 3b; see Joel 4:17 [3:17]; compare Isa 1:21-26; Ezek 48:35).

The second oracle (vv. 4-5) is introduced with a traditional formula (v. 4a). It specifies two groups of persons who will revel in the Lord's presence. "Old men and old women" (v. 4b) and "boys and girls" (v. 5) will fill the streets of the city and enjoy their activities without fear (see Amos 5:16; Lam 2:11-12; Isa 65:20; Ps 127:3-4; Jer 30:18-21). The two groups are described in harmony and sexual equality. They represent those who would have found the journey back from exile quite difficult. The groups also reverse the anxiety about the present depopulation of the temple-community (see 7:14; compare 7:7).

streets. ⁶Thus says the LORD of hosts: Even if this should seem impossible in the eyes of the remnant of this people, shall it in those days be impossible in my eyes also, says the LORD of hosts? ⁷Thus says the LORD of hosts: Lo, I will rescue my people from the land of the rising sun, and from the land of the setting sun. ⁸I will bring them back to dwell within Jerusalem. They shall be my people, and I will be their God, with faithfulness and justice.

⁹Thus says the LORD of hosts: Let your hands be strong, you who in these days hear these words spoken by the prophets on the day when the foundation of the house of the LORD of hosts was laid for the building of the temple. ¹⁰For before those days there were no wages for men, or hire for beasts; those who came and went had no security from the enemy, for I set every man against his neighbor. ¹¹But now I will not deal with the remnant of

The third oracle (v. 6) is introduced as the first two oracles were (v. 6a). It presents God's rhetorical question about the expectations of the community toward divine activity (v. 6b). Does the reversal of present circumstances, that is, depopulated city, "remnant" group (see Hag 1:12), appear impossible? (compare Gen 28:14; Jer 32:17, 27).

God reassures the community in the fourth oracle (vv. 7-8). After the introduction (v. 7a), God promises to repopulate the city by delivering the exiles from captivity (v. 7b). The "land of the rising sun . . . of the setting sun" refers to Babylon and Egypt (compare 2:10 [2:6]; Jer 31:8). The exiles will share God's dwelling in Jerusalem (v. 8).

"They shall be my people, and I will be their God" indicates that the covenant contracted by their ancestors remains a reality for those returning (v. 8b; see Lev 26:12; Jer 31:33). The phrase "with faithfulness and justice" suggests God's response to the covenant as well as the challenge of mutuality for the community in maintaining the covenant.

8:9-17 Encouragement and challenge for Jerusalem. The section is comprised of two parts (vv. 9-13 and 14-17). Each begins with a traditional prophetic formula as an introduction (vv. 9a, 14a). Each presents past tragedy and develops future possibilities of blessing. Both refer to earlier ethical teaching as well as to earlier verses in First Zechariah.

After the introduction (v. 9a), the first exhortation is "let your hands be strong." The addressees are those who had heard Haggai speak about the necessity of temple restoration, especially the "foundation of the house of the Lord." The term "prophets" suggests that the addressees of that prophet had also heard Zechariah, who was Haggai's contemporary (v. 9b; see Hag 1:6-11; 2:15-19).

Verse 10 describes the situation before temple restoration began in earnest. At that time there was no economic security (v. 10a). In addition, hostile forces precluded security. God initiated the circumstances by setting each person against the neighbor (v. 10b).

this people as in former days, says the LORD of hosts, ¹²for it is the seedtime of peace: the vine shall yield its fruit, the land shall bear its crops, and the heavens shall give their dew; all these things I will have the remnant of the people possess. ¹³Just as you were a curse among the nations, O house of Judah and house of Israel, so will I save you that you may be a blessing; do not fear, but let your hands be strong.

¹⁴Thus says the LORD of hosts: As I determined to harm you when your fathers provoked me to wrath, says the LORD of hosts, and I did not relent, ¹⁵so again in these days I have determined to favor Jerusalem and the house of Judah; do not fear! ¹⁶These then are the things you should do: Speak the truth to one another; let there be honesty and peace in the judgments at your gates, ¹⁷and let none of you plot evil against another in his heart, nor love a false oath. For all these things I hate, says the LORD.

¹⁸This word of the LORD of hosts came to me: ¹⁹Thus says the LORD of hosts: The fast days of the fourth, the fifth, the seventh, and the tenth months shall become occasions of joy and gladness, cheerful festivals for the house of Judah;

Verse 11 introduces a new oracle. God's judgment is reversed. God will act differently: "But now I will not deal with the remnant of this people as in former days . . . ." The expression is similar to covenant language. How will the present situation be different for the temple-community? It is described as "the seedtime of peace," that is, vine and land will be productive; the heavens will water the earth (v. 12a; compare Hag 1:10-11).

Another contrast concludes the first part. As Israel and Judah were "a curse among the nations," now they will be a "blessing" through God's saving intervention (v. 13a; see v. 7b). The oracle concludes with two exhortations: "do not fear, but let your hands be strong" (v. 12b; compare Deut 28:1-28). The second exhortation forms an inclusion with verse 9b, formally closing the oracle.

The second part begins with an introduction to another oracle (v. 14a). The construction "as . . . so" provides the structure for comparing past history and present experience (vv. 14b-15; see 1:6; 7:13). It also repeats previous oracles. As God had decided to harm the community because of its ancestral history and "did not relent" (v. 14b; see 1:6b; compare Jer 4:28; 51:12; Lam 2:17), so God decided "in these days . . . to favor Jerusalem and the house of Judah" (v. 15).

The oracle concludes with a short summary of ethical teaching about truth and honesty in judgments (compare 7:9); exhortations against evil plans for others (compare 7:10b) and against false oaths (compare 5:3-4). God detests these activities (vv. 16-17).

8:18-23 Responses about fasting and the future. Two oracles conclude First Zechariah. The first one (vv. 18-19) responds to the delegation's question about fasting (7:2-3), while the second is a description of the role of Jerusalem for the temple-community and the nations.

only love faithfulness and peace. 20Thus says the LORD of hosts: There shall yet come peoples, the inhabitants of many cities, 21and the inhabitants of one city shall approach those of another, and say, "Come! let us go to implore the favor of the LORD"; and, "I too will go to seek the LORD." 22Many peoples and strong nations shall come to seek the LORD of hosts in Jerusalem and to implore the favor of the LORD. 23Thus says the LORD of hosts: In those days ten men of every nationality, speaking different tongues, shall take hold, yes, take hold of every Jew by the edge of his garment and say, "Let us go with you, for we have heard that God is with you."

A prophetic formula introduces the first oracle (v. 18). The phrase "to me" is added to indicate that the response to the delegation is mediated through Zechariah and not the priests (see 7:3). The decision begins with a listing of traditional times of fasting: "the fourth, the fifth, the seventh and the tenth months" (v. 19a).

Compared to the other notations (see 7:3b, 5b), two months are added. The significance for these days of the months is identical with the other months' commemoration: the tragic events leading to the destruction of Jerusalem. The fourth month commemorates the Babylonian attack on the walls (see 2 Kgs 25:3-7; Jer 39:2), while the tenth month marks the beginning of the siege of Jerusalem (see 1 Kgs 25:1-2; Jer 39:1).

Verse 19b dramatically reverses the commemorative status of the collective days of the four months. The days previously given to mourning and fasting are designated as "occasions of joy and gladness, cheerful festivals for the house of Judah" (v. 19b). The expressions in Hebrew identify times of celebratory banquets (see Esth 8:16-17); happiness at social festivities (1 Sam 18:6; 1 Kgs 1:40; Isa 9:2); and happy assemblies for cultic activity (Isa 33:20).

The addition "only love faithfulness and peace" (v. 19c; RSV: "truth and peace") stipulates qualities of living. "Truth," in particular, attends to how community members are challenged to interact with one another and how they regard one another (see vv. 16-17). Can the community be commanded to love truth and peace? The oracle states a promise for a better future if the community responds according to this norm (compare Deut 6:4-5; Amos 5:4; 6).

A prophetic formula introduces the second oracle (v. 20a). "Peoples, the inhabitants of many cities" (v. 20b), will approach Jerusalem (compare 2:11; Isa 2:2-4; 66:18-21; Mic 4:1-3). There will be a mutual interaction among them as they invite one another to approach (v. 21a). The same motivations of the delegation to approach Jerusalem (see 7:2-3) characterize the city-dwellers: "Come! let us go to implore the favor of the Lord . . . I, too, will go to seek the Lord" (v. 21b).

Verse 22 reiterates verse 21b by forming a *chiastic* structure, a literary device resembling an X. The first clause of verse 21b parallels the last clause of verse 22, forming the left stroke of the X. Likewise, the second clause of verse 21b parallels the first clause of verse 22, forming the right stroke of the X.

Verse 23 continues the notion of the repopulated city drawn from persons of the Diaspora and the nations. "Ten men of every nationality" refers to a number of completeness and the number needed to constitute a prayer grouping (v. 23a). What is even more remarkable is how these persons of different nationalities and tongues "shall take hold of every Jew by the edge of his garment and say, 'Let us go with you, for we have heard that God is with you'" (v. 23b).

The term "Jew" appears only in verse 23 and Jer 34:9. Some suggest that the role of invitation to approach Jerusalem gives the Diaspora Jews a significant role. Others find the expression a missionary statement. The proclamation "we have heard that God is with you" is the fulfillment of God's promise to the temple-community: "Return to me . . . and I will return to you" (1:3). The role of the community is twofold: to live with integrity and hasten the return of the Lord to Jerusalem; and to invite others to share in the Lord's blessings by approaching and residing in the city where God dwells.

Conclusion

First Zechariah, like Haggai, has been assessed according to the criterion of unfulfilled prophecy. The perspective is deceptive. It limits any contribution of the prophet to his contemporaries and subsequent communities of believers. When one evaluates the text according to literary form, redaction, and closely aligned religious insights, however, the prophet stands as an exemplary source of how to construct and discover meaning in the process of restoration.

Zechariah, like Haggai, had a few common goals. This is to be expected, since they functioned separately but as contemporaries.

a) Both encouraged efforts at temple reconstruction. Bleak conditions challenged their vision of the future importance of the temple. Its completion would symbolize the restoration of the community's relationship with God. God's presence would provide a new community identity.

b) The prophets proclaimed a necessary ethical component for the restoration of relationship with God and the continuance of this relationship. Yet neither prophet proposed a simple cause-effect relationship between human effort and God's response. They lived in the mystery of the faithful God who continued to reveal mercy within the community through "glory (*kabod*)" and "spirit (*ruach*)."

c) Leadership in the community was shared. Zerubbabel was a clear candidate for leadership, since he symbolized the restoration of a Davidic figure and stability to the returned exiles.

First Zechariah also contributes individual insights through the complex "night" visions and interpretive oracles:

a) The visions witness to his broad experience of God, whose presence is not limited to Jerusalem. Interesting characters, angels, and an interpreting assistant interact with him to provide a rich understanding of how and why God continues to be with the temple-community. The oracles added by a final editor bridge the distance between the experience of Zechariah and the interpretation necessary for later communities to understand that experience.

b) The visions are characterized by an indefinite geography, fluidity of movement, and solitary or frequent occurrence through "all the earth." No longer is Israel isolated in its efforts at restoration. The cosmos participates and supports the struggle. This dimension adds mystery and awe to the situation of "in betweenness," that is, a time between promises of a new community proclaimed during the Exile (see Isa 40–55; Ezek 40–48) and fulfillment for the recently returned exiles.

c) The visions are directed to "theological" concerns, that is, God's presence, restored ritual, and purity. God, however, is no longer localized in the temple but is described as "glory" and "a wall of fire" for the community. Restored ritual is dependent upon the purity of the high priest and the integrity of the community.

There is also a close correspondence between these concerns and other factors, including leadership, punishment of evil community members, and the future population of Jerusalem. Leadership is to be equally shared by civic and religious authorities, who assist God in the directives for the new community. "Curses" mete out punishment to those who are irresponsible toward one another. Possibilities of urban dwellers to populate Jerusalem are dependent on the cooperation of the Diaspora Jews.

SECOND ZECHARIAH

Zech 9:1–14:21

The reader is invited to follow the suggestions outlined in the introduction to the Book of Zechariah (see p. 58). Reviewing sections of the introduction and preliminary considerations for First and Second Zechariah will provide a clearer context for the commentary on Second Zechariah.

Authorship

There is no indication of authorship. Although the earliest manuscript of the Minor Prophets from Qumran shows no break between Zech 1–8 and 9–14, modern scholarship does not agree that both parts originated from one author. The history of scholarship from the early 1700's, which includes the linguistic analysis of the past decade, offers the same conclusions.

Three arguments against the unity of authorship are presented:

a) The *content* of First Zechariah, which is concerned with temple reconstruction, historical figures, and dated oracles, contrasts with the material of Second Zechariah, which addresses God's judgments and "eschatological" promises (promises about God's future action). The historical context is obscure.

b) The *style* is considerably different. First Zechariah is a compilation of "night" visions and interpretive oracles written in prose, while Second Zechariah is a series of oracles derived from reference to earlier prophets and written in poetry. First-person references of the prophet are absent.

c) The *vocabulary* is different in introducing oracles. First Zechariah uses traditional prophetic formulas, whereas Second Zechariah uses the phrase "An oracle: The word of the Lord" to introduce the two major sections (9:1; 12:1). The vocabulary of Second Zechariah, like the style, is dependent on earlier prophets.

Dating of the text

There are no verses that contain any specific dates. Possibilities for identifying a historical context are dependent upon internal clues:

a) The use of preexilic and exilic prophecy (Isaiah, Hosea, Jeremiah, Ezekiel, Joel), as well as themes characteristic of Joel, for example "day of the Lord," indicates a postexilic context.

b) Some allusions to events that occur after 333 B.C.E. appear especially in chapter 9 (see the commentary on ch. 9).

c) Apocalyptic style and content, especially in chapter 14, suggest a period later than the early postexilic that characterizes First Zechariah.

The consensus among scholars is to date the text after the conquest of Alexander the Great (333 B.C.E.) and within two decades following his formation of the new empire. The final date for the editorial process of First and Second Zechariah is before 200 B.C.E. There is no agreement, however, about the number of editors, the extent of redaction, and the length of time required for the canonical shaping of Zechariah.

Composition of the text

How the oracles were ordered and edited is unknown. Scholars propose that two units of material, each three chapters long, were arranged with common superscriptions: "An oracle: the word of the Lord" (9:1; 12:1). The same superscription appears in Mal 1:1. The two units of Second Zechariah were appended to First Zechariah because of a perceived relationship. The fourteen chapters became the eleventh Minor Prophet. The one unit of Malachi was added to the other prophetic scrolls, thus constituting the Twelve Minor Prophets (see p. 7).

There are several problem verses in Second Zechariah due to the poetic language. Less rearrangement of Second Zechariah is suggested than for First Zechariah. The New English Bible is the only translation that suggests the following order: 9:1–11:17; 13:7-9; 12:1-14; 13:1-6; 14:1-21.

Outline of the text

PART ONE:	First Oracle: Judgments of God (9:1–11:17)
9:1a	Superscription
9:1b-8	Invasion by the Lord
9:9-10	Coming of the King
9:11–10:1	Victory for the Community
10:2–11:3	Shepherd Oracles
11:4-17	Shepherd Allegory
PART TWO:	Second Oracle: Restoration (12:1–14:21)
12:1	Superscription
12:2-9	Jerusalem and Judah
12:10–13:1	Mourning in Jerusalem
13:2-6	Purification in Jerusalem
13:7-9	Sword and Fire
14:1	Superscription
14:2-5	War and Victory
14:6-11	Transformation of Land
14:12-15	Plague and Tumult
14:16-21	Celebration in Jerusalem

Invasion by the Lord

9 An oracle:
The word of the LORD is upon the land of Hadrach,
and Damascus is its resting place,
For the cities of Aram are the LORD's,
as are all the tribes of Israel,
[2]Hamath also, on its border,
Tyre, too, and Sidon, however wise they be.

[3]Tyre built herself a stronghold,
and heaped up silver like dust,
and gold like the mire of the streets.
[4]Lo, the LORD will strip her of her possessions,
and smite her power on the sea,
and she shall be devoured by fire.
[5]Ashkelon shall see it and be afraid;
Gaza also: she shall be in great anguish;

PART ONE: JUDGMENTS OF GOD

Zech 9:1–11:17

Part One is an interweaving of God's judgments: destruction and restoration. All judgments are future-oriented. Unlike the future proposed by First Zechariah, however, this future appears closer and virtually imminent. There is one theme that indicates development among the edited oracles. It is the contrast between the leadership that genuine and false shepherds exercise over the community.

9:1a Superscription. The wording of the superscription, "An oracle: the word of the Lord," has already been noted (see pp. 89, 90). The translation is common to most versions. The Hebrew, however, specifies the first word as "burden."

As an introduction to the first and second oracles (9:1–11:17; 11:1–14:21), the superscription suggests that a particular responsibility has been given to the prophet on behalf of God's people. Since the first oracle is equally concerned with God's judgments of destruction and restoration, the unknown prophet might well hesitate to proclaim God's message. Yet God's word must be announced as it was received.

The rest of the superscription directs the Lord's word to "the land of Hadrach, and Damascus is its resting place" (9:1a). Although Hadrach does not occur in the Old Testament, archeological data locates it in Syria north of Hamath (v. 2). Damascus, the capital, is located in central Syria. What is the relationship of God's word to this country? The translation "against the land" suggests God's negative judgment toward Syria, especially Damascus, a traditional enemy (see Amos 1:2).

9:1b-8 Invasion by the Lord. Verse 1b describes additional "cities of Aram" and "all the tribes of Israel" as belonging to the Lord. Verse 1 proclaims God's judgment against northern cities that belong to God just as Israel does. Verses 2 and 3 enumerate additional cities under God's judgment: Hamath (in Syria), Tyre and Sidon (south along the seacoast). Some commentators

Ekron, too, for her hope shall come to nought.
The king shall disappear from Gaza, and Ashkelon shall not be inhabited,
6 and the baseborn shall occupy Ashdod.
I will destroy the pride of the Philistine
7 and take from his mouth his bloody meat,
and his abominations from between his teeth;
He also shall become a remnant for our God,
and shall be like a family in Judah, and Ekron shall be like the Jebusites.
8I will encamp by my house as a guard that none may pass to and fro;

No oppressor shall pass over them again,
for now I have regard for their affliction.

Restoration under the Messiah

9Rejoice heartily, O daughter Zion, shout for joy, O daughter Jerusalem!
See, your king shall come to you; a just savior is he,
Meek, and riding on an ass, on a colt, the foal of an ass.
10He shall banish the chariot from Ephraim,
and the horse from Jerusalem;
The warrior's bow shall be banished, and he shall proclaim peace to the nations.

identify the cities (vv. 1-7) as those conquered by Alexander as he destroyed the Persian empire and promised a new age. Alexander may have raised hopes for the messianic age as he conquered Israel's enemies.

The wisdom and riches connected with Tyre and Sidon (vv. 2b-3) will be useless against the Lord's attack and destruction "by fire" (v. 4). Other southern cities, such as Ashkelon, Gaza, Ekron, will witness the consequences and respond with fear, anguish, and despair. The king will flee, as will the inhabitants, and the "baseborn will occupy Ashdod" (vv. 4b-6a; see Neh 13:24).

A grammatical change to first person singular (v. 6a) heightens the role of the Lord in the invasion. God will intervene to destroy the pride of the Philistines and their abominable sacrifices. Nonetheless, even the Philistines will become part of God's "remnant" and will be "like a family in Judah" (v. 7). The final note promises the Lord's protection for all who will live in Jerusalem, "my house." The designation of the trespassers and the promise of the Lord's watching parallel two passages of First Zechariah (see 7:14 and 4:10b).

9:9-10 Coming of the king. The transformation of God's judgment of destruction to restoration noted in the previous section may be the context for the description of the future king (vv. 9-10). Exhortations to rejoice and shout for joy are addressed to the community named "daughter Zion . . . daughter Jerusalem" (v. 9a; compare Zech 2:10).

The king will be "a just savior . . . meek, and riding . . . on a colt" (v. 9b; compare Matt 21:5; John 12:15). Most commentators identify the figure as a messianic king who is "just," one actively involved in all aspects of vindication. He is "meek" in his corresponding role as "servant" (com-

His dominion shall be from sea to sea,
and from the River to the ends of the
earth.
¹¹As for you, for the blood of your covenant with me,
I will bring forth your prisoners from
the dungeon.
¹²In the return to the fortress
of the waiting prisoners,
This very day, I will return you
double for your exile.
¹³For I will bend Judah as my bow,
I will arm myself with Ephraim;
I will arouse your sons, O Zion,
[against your sons, O Yavan,]

and I will use you as a warrior's
sword.
¹⁴The LORD shall appear over them,
and his arrow shall shoot forth as
lightning;
The LORD God shall sound the trumpet,
and come in a storm from the south.
¹⁵The LORD of hosts shall be a shield over
them,
they shall overcome sling stones
and trample them underfoot;
They shall drink blood like wine,
till they are filled with it like libation
bowls,
like the corners of the altar.

pare Isa 49:4; 50:8; 53:12). Riding on a colt was a custom of officials (see Gen 49:10-11; Judg 5:10; 1 Kgs 1:33).

Again a grammatical change to first person singular (see v. 6a) emphasizes the Lord's role. All implements of war will be banished: chariot, horse, warrior's bow (v. 10a). Reconciliation of the northern (Ephraim) and southern (Jerusalem) kingdoms issues forth in "peace to the nations" and worldwide "dominion" (v. 10b; compare Ps 78:7-8).

9:11-10:1 Victory for the community. The section consists of three oracles joined by word associations. The images of return, "theophany," that is, God's manifestation, and restoration of the community and land are highlighted. Earlier history and references to ideas in Second Isaiah are bases for the development of the section.

The grammatical change to first person indicates a new oracle (vv. 11-13). Israel is addressed directly: "As for you, for the blood of your covenant with me . . ." (v. 11a; see Exod 24:8; compare Mark 14:24). The relationship prompts the Lord to initiate a rescue of prisoners from the dungeon of exile (vv. 11-12a; compare Isa 42:7; 61:1b). The exile experience will be reversed: "This very day I will return you double" (v. 12b; compare Isa 40:2; 61:7).

Those who captured Israel will be judged by the captives. Verse 13, which concludes the section, describes how Judah and Ephraim (the totality of Israel) will be as a bow and arrow (RSV) for God's judgment against their enemies (compare Ps 7:13-14). They will be as a "warrior's sword" against "your sons, O Yavan." Although Yavan occurs in the Old Testament to indicate the Greeks (see Gen 10:2, 4; Isa 66:19; Joel 4:4 [3:3]), it probably was added here during the Maccabean era (ca. 167 B.C.E.) to point to current oppressors of Israel.

¹⁶And the LORD, their God, shall save
   them on that day,
his people, like a flock.
For they are the jewels in a crown
   raised aloft over his land.
¹⁷For what wealth is theirs, and what
   beauty!
grain that makes the youths flourish,
and new wine, the maidens!

The New Order of Things

10 ¹Ask of the LORD rain in the
   spring season!

It is the LORD who makes the storm
   clouds,
And sends men the pouring rain;
   for everyone, grassy fields.
²For the teraphim speak nonsense,
   the diviners have false visions:
Deceitful dreams they tell,
   empty comfort they offer.
This is why they wander like sheep,
   wretched: they have no shepherd.
³My wrath is kindled against the shepherds,
and I will punish the leaders;

The role of the Lord as a victorious warrior (vv. 14-15) is the second oracle of the section. It draws on the concept of the holy war (see the commentary on Joel 2:1-11; compare Pss 18:7-15; 77:16-20). The images of lightning, trumpet, and storm correspond to God's theophany on Mount Sinai (v. 14; compare Exod 24:9-10, 15, 18). God protects the covenanted community as they engage in the battle, overcoming and trampling their enemies (v. 15a; see 2 Sam 22:8-18). The victory is described as a sacrificial ritual (v. 15b; Exod 24:6-8; compare Lev 16:14-15; 17:11).

The victory for the community is described in the third oracle (9:16–10:1). God will save the people, who are "like a flock" and "jewels in a crown raised aloft over his land" (v. 16; compare Zech 6:14). Abundance of grain, new wine, rain, and grassy fields indicates a restored community and land (9:17–10:1; see Joel 2:19, 22-24; compare Hag 1:10-11; 2:19).

10:2–11:3 Shepherd oracles. This section and the following one (11:4-17) provide different images of shepherds. The theme constitutes over fifty percent of the first oracle (9:1–11:17). Again, the oracles are separated by third-person and first-person grammatical changes. Themes of genuine leadership, restoration, and punishment for Israel's enemies are used.

The Lord speaks (vv. 2-5). Verse 2 is a transition connecting the theme of "grassy fields" for "everyone" (v. 1b) to the shepherd and sheep theme (v. 2b). "Diviners" have duped the community, utilizing "teraphim" or household gods (see Judg 17:5; 18:5) for future speculations, which God judges as "nonsense," "false visions," "deceitful dreams," and "empty comfort" (v. 2a; compare Jer 23:32; 27:9). Many commentators think use of the teraphim was limited to the preexilic period and the chaotic condition of the community before the Exile. To some extent, they were also used in the postexilic community (compare Mal 3:5a; Isa 65:3-5; 66:17).

Earlier tradition claims that treacherous leadership led the community astray (see Hos 4:4-9; Mic 3; Jer 2:26). The shepherd as leader had been a

For the LORD of hosts will visit his flock,
the house of Judah,
and make them his stately war horse.
⁴From him shall come leader and chief,
from him warrior's bow and every officer.
⁵They shall all be warriors,
trampling the mire of the streets in
battle;
They shall wage war because the LORD
is with them,
and shall put the horsemen to rout.

⁶I will strengthen the house of Judah,
the house of Joseph I will save;
I will bring them back, because I have
mercy on them,
they shall be as though I had never
cast them off,
for I am the LORD, their God, and I
will hear them.
⁷Then Ephraim shall be valiant men,
and their hearts shall be cheered as by
wine.
Their children shall see it and be glad,
their hearts shall rejoice in the LORD.

personal symbol of Hammurabi (1728–1686 B.C.E.). Later "shepherd" was used to designate God (see Gen 49:24; Ps 23), as was "just king" (see Isa 44:28; Jer 23:2-4; Mic 5:4; Ezek 34:23-24).

"Shepherds" and "leaders" are parallel terms and the objects of God's wrath (v. 3a). The verb states that God "visits" different persons, God's visitation "will punish the leaders," but the visitation of the flock results in making them a "stately war horse" (v. 3b). The flock, identified as the house of Judah, is the context for the development of the victor-warrior in verses 4-5 (see 9:11–10:1).

Verses 4 and 5 list a number of traditional metaphors which indicate the type of leadership that will come forth from Judah ("from him"—v. 4). The Revised Standard Version and the New English Bible render the sense of the Hebrew better than the New American Bible for both verses. In verse 4a three metaphors occur: "cornerstone" (NAB: "leader") indicates stability (see Judg 20:2; 1 Sam 14:38; compare Ps 118:22); "tent peg" (NAB: "chief") suggests endurance (see Isa 22:23); "warrior's bow" (NAB also) suggests fearless courage (see 2 Kgs 13:17; compare Rev 6:2). Verse 5 identifies the leaders as "warriors" who will be victorious: "the Lord is with them . . . ."

The second oracle, a composite of several divine proclamations, develops the theme of restoration (vv. 6-12). Verse 6 concludes the focus on Judah by noting God's activities of strengthening and saving Judah and the "house of Joseph," that is, the northern kingdom (v. 6a). Judah and Joseph will be brought back and treated with mercy (see Jer 33:26; compare Hos 11; Zech 7:13). A wonderful expression describes the new situation: "They shall be as though I had never cast them off . . . ." (v. 6b).

Verses 7-9 reveal the future of Ephraim (the northern kingdom). As "valiant warriors" (RSV; see Judg 7:24-25; 8:1-3) with cheerful hearts, their children will witness them and "be glad . . . and rejoice in the Lord" (v. 7; compare Isa 29:19). The Lord will bring them back from exile with a "whistle,"

⁸I will whistle for them to come together,
  and when I redeem them
  they will be as numerous as before.
⁹I sowed them among the nations,
  yet in distant lands they remember
    me;
  they shall rear their children and re-
    turn.
¹⁰I will bring them back from the land of
    Egypt,
  and gather them from Assyria.
  I will bring them into Gilead and into
    Lebanon,
  but these shall not suffice them;
¹¹I will cross over to Egypt
  and smite the waves of the sea
  and all the depths of the Nile shall be
    dried up.

The pride of Assyria shall be cast down,
  and the scepter of Egypt taken away.
¹²I will strengthen them in the Lord,
  and they shall walk in his name,
  says the Lord.

11 ¹Open your doors, O Lebanon,
  that the fire may devour your
    cedars!
²Wail, you cypress trees,
  for the cedars are fallen,
  the mighty have been despoiled.
  Wail, you oaks of Bashan,
  for the impenetrable forest is cut
    down!
³Hark! the wailing of the shepherds,
  their glory has been ruined.
  Hark! the roaring of the young lions,
  the jungle of the Jordan is laid waste.

that is, a signal. It is an ironic expression first used to denote God's "signal" to Israel's enemies (compare Isa 5:26-30). Ephraim will experience the past in a new way (v. 8a; compare v. 6b). Although scattered "among the nations," they "remember" the Lord and "rear their children and return" (v. 9).

Verses 10-12 continue the theme of restoration of the exiles. Egypt and Assyria were countries involved in the destruction of the northern and southern kingdoms (see Isa 7:18). Gilead and Lebanon are fertile, rich areas ideal for restoration. In Egypt, the Nile will dry up and the scepter will be taken away. In Assyria, "pride . . . will be cast down" (v. 11). For those returning from exile, however, God's strength will enable them to continue home (v. 12; compare v. 6; Isa 40:31).

The final section is a "taunt song" against the treacherous shepherds (11:1-3). The literary form was used by earlier prophets to proclaim God's judgment on Israel's enemies (see 5:2; Isa 14:4-21; Jer 6:1-5). Here the enemies of Israel are compared to trees, and their leaders are shepherds (compare Isa 10:33-34; Ezek 31). Lebanon and Bashan are particularly singled out for judgment; they were often linked together in earlier prophecy (see Isa 2:13; Jer 22:20; Ezek 27:5-6).

Lebanon is addressed first: cedars and cypress are destroyed, devastating the wealth of the area (vv. 1-2a). Cedar was a symbol of the royal house of Judah (see Ezek 17:3, 4, 12f.). Next Bashan is considered: "the impenetrable forest is cut down!" (v. 2b). The different trees symbolize various nations. Finally the shepherds lament, for "their glory has been ruined" (v. 3a). "The roaring of the young lions" may suggest other leaders whose territory

Allegory of the Shepherds. ⁴Thus said the Lᴏʀᴅ, my God: Shepherd the flock to be slaughtered. ⁵For they who buy them slay them with impunity; while those who sell them say, "Blessed be the Lᴏʀᴅ, I have become rich!" Even their own shepherds do not feel for them. ⁶(Nor shall I spare the inhabitants of the earth any more, says the Lᴏʀᴅ. Yes, I will deliver each of them into the power of his neighbor, or into the power of his king; they shall crush the earth, and I will not deliver it out of their power.)

⁷So I became the shepherd of the flock to be slaughtered for the sheep merchants. I took two staffs, one of which I called "Favor," and the other, "Bonds," and I fed the flock. ⁸In a single month I did away with the three shepherds. I wearied of them, and they behaved badly toward me. ⁹"I will not feed you," I said. "What is to die, let it die; what is to perish, let

is devastated "in the jungle of the Jordan" (v. 3b; compare Jer 25:34-37; 50:44; Ezek 19:1-9).

11:4-17 Shepherd allegory. This section is prose except for verse 17, which is poetry. While the themes of shepherd and sheep have been noted above (see 9:16; 10:2, 3, 8-9; 11:3), they are most developed here. Oracles in the first person contain three symbolic acts. Most commentators interpret the section as allegory, proposing that the symbolic acts are a written imitation of earlier prophetic tradition. The section is divided into three parts: verses 4-6; 7-14; 15-17.

The superscription of the first oracle (vv. 4-6) is unusual (v. 4a). The phrase "my God," found in many prayers (see Pss 7:2; 18:3; 22:2; 88:2), suggests a separation of the speaker from the hearers (see Joel 1:3; Josh 9:23). The prophet may be initiating controversy both through use of the phrase as well as through his self-identification as the shepherd of the flock (v. 4b).

The prophet uses the image of a market with buyers and sellers of sheep to condemn the leaders with Israel. The buyers—foreign nations that occupied Israel—"slay them with impunity," while the sellers—religious leaders *within* Israel—"do not even feel for them" (v. 5; compare Amos 2:6; Jer 38:8-22; Neh 5:10-13). God's judgment mirrors the conduct of the shepherds. Neither leaders nor people will be delivered by God (v. 6b).

The second oracle (vv. 7-14) contrasts the prophet as leader with previous leaders (vv. 4-6). Verse 7 parallels verse 4b. The Lord's command to "shepherd the flock" (v. 4b) is obeyed by the prophet, who is employed by the sheep merchants (v. 7a). Staffs in hand, the prophet "fed the flock" (v. 7b).

Verse 8a is a gloss whose meaning is unclear. Who are the "three shepherds"? How did they function? At least forty interpretations have been suggested in the past century. Since there is little information about what transpired in the Jewish community between 350–200 B.C.E. (see p. 10), it is believed that the three shepherds may have functioned during that time either as high priests or as temple officials.

it perish, and let those that are left devour one another's flesh."

¹⁰Then I took my staff "Favor" and snapped it asunder, breaking off the covenant which I had made with all peoples; ¹¹that day it was broken off. The sheep merchants who were watching me understood that this was the word of the LORD. ¹²I said to them, "If it seems good to you, give me my wages; but if not, let it go." And they counted out my wages, thirty pieces of silver. ¹³But the LORD said to me, "Throw it in the treasury, the handsome price at which they valued me." So I took the thirty pieces of silver and threw them into the treasury in the house of the LORD.

¹⁴Then I snapped asunder my other staff, "Bonds," breaking off the brotherhood between Judah and Israel. ¹⁵The LORD said to me: This time take the gear of a foolish shepherd. ¹⁶For I will raise up a shepherd in the land who will take no note of those that perish, nor seek the strays, nor heal the injured, nor feed what survives—he will eat the flesh of the fat ones and tear off their hoofs!

¹⁷Woe to my foolish shepherd
who forsakes the flock!
May the sword fall upon his arm
and upon his right eye;
Let his arm wither away entirely,
and his right eye be blind forever!

Verse 8b resumes the narrative and indicates the mutual dissatisfaction of shepherd (prophet) and flock (undetermined). The prophet's rejection impels him to withhold leadership from the people. He leaves them to their own resources (v. 9).

The next response of the prophet is to "snap asunder" both staffs. Verses 10 and 14 function as an inclusion for verses 11-13. The literary structure is similar to the "vision within the vision" (see the commentary on 4:1-6a; 10b-14; 6b-10a). Verse 10 describes the prophet's action of breaking his first staff, called "Favor," and interprets it as "breaking off the covenant which I had made with all peoples." The implication is that gentile nations as well had contracted a covenant with God. The second staff, called "Union," is also broken, which is interpreted as "breaking off the brotherhood of Judah and Israel" (v. 14), the period of the divided kingdom before and after the Exile.

The second symbolic act is described in verses 11-13. The prophet indicates through his action that in rejecting him, the people have rejected God (compare Matt 27:4-6). In Hebrew, "treasury" is also translated "to the potter." Artisans worked in the temple area to provide clay receptacles for the treasury, which held sacred objects and served as a bank for private holdings (2 Macc 3:10ff.; compare Matt 27:6-9).

The third oracle (vv. 15-17) includes a command of the Lord to the prophet to perform a third symbolic act. Although the description of the act is omitted, its significance is emphasized: "God will raise up" an utterly incompetent shepherd unconcerned that the flock will "perish," "stray," need healing or food (v. 16a). Who is the foolish shepherd? Again, the verse defies a clear

12 **Jerusalem God's Instrument.** ¹An oracle: the word of the LORD concerning Israel. Thus says the LORD, who spreads out the heavens, lays the foundations of the earth, and forms the spirit of man within him: ²See, I will make Jerusalem a bowl to stupefy all peoples round about. [Judah will be besieged, even Jerusalem.] ³On that day I will make Jerusalem a weighty stone for all peoples. All who attempt to lift it shall injure themselves badly, and all the nations of the earth shall be gathered against her. ⁴On that day, says the LORD, I will strike

historical context. Some commentators suggest the office of high priest (compare Ezek 34:1-6).

The allegory concludes with a poetic "woe" imprecation to the "foolish shepherd who forsakes the flock" (v. 17a). Curses of a useless arm and blind eye will render the shepherd incompetent and unable to lead (v. 17b).

PART TWO: RESTORATION

Zech 12:1–14:21

Part Two is a collection of edited oracles about God's restoration of the temple-community. Future battles, purification, and blessings will occur "on that day" for the community as well as for the nations. The collection may have been added to restore communal hope after Alexander's career did not fulfill messianic expectations. Part Two, especially chapter 14, contains more proto-apocalyptic characteristics than Part One (see pp. 15, 59).

12:1 Superscription. "An oracle: the word of the Lord" repeats 9:1 and introduces Part Two (see p. 90). The phrase "concerning Israel" was probably added by an editor, since Israel is not mentioned again. It may, however, refer to all the inhabitants of Israel (see 1 Chr 21:1; 2 Chr 29:24). Verse 1b is a new introduction: "Thus says the Lord." The description that follows identifies the Lord as creator, similar to other hymnic identifications (see Isa 40:22; 42:5; Ps 24:1-2).

12:2-9 Jerusalem and Judah. This section is a series of divine oracles proclaimed in the first person. The creator God promises prominence to Jerusalem and Judah as victorious over the nations. Traditional metaphors are used frequently. The phrase "on that day" occurs in five verses of chapter 12 (sixteen times in chapters 12–14).

The first oracle is constructed in perfect parallelism (vv. 2-3). God will make "Jerusalem . . . a bowl . . . and a weighty stone for all peoples roundabout" (vv. 2a, 3a). Both will thwart enemies: "stupefy . . . injure themselves badly" (vv. 2b, 3b). The bowl is a symbol of God's wrath toward Israel's enemies (see Jer 25:15-16; Ezek 23:31-34; compare Isa 51:17), while the weighty stone indicates an unmovable barrier for the enemy (see Isa

99

every horse with fright, and its rider with madness. I will strike blind all the horses of the peoples, but upon the house of Judah I will open my eyes, ⁵and the princes of Judah shall say to themselves, "The inhabitants of Jerusalem have their strength in the LORD of hosts, their God." ⁶On that day I will make the princes of Judah like a brazier of fire in the woodland, and like a burning torch among sheaves, and they shall devour right and left all the surrounding peoples; but Jerusalem shall still abide on its own site.

⁷The LORD shall save the tents of Judah first, that the glory of the house of David and the glory of the inhabitants of Jerusalem may not be exalted over Judah. ⁸On that day, the LORD will shield the inhabitants of Jerusalem, and the weakling among them shall be like David on that day, and the house of David godlike, like an angel of the Lord before them. ⁹On that day I will seek the destruction of all nations that come against Jerusalem.

Messianic Jerusalem. ¹⁰I will pour out on the house of David and on the inhabi-

8:14-15; 28:16; compare Zech 3:9). "For all peoples roundabout" is a repetition of Joel 4:11-12 [3:11-12].

The second oracle presents the Lord as the victorious warrior on behalf of Judah and Jerusalem (vv. 4-5). The third oracle describes the "clans of Judah" taking a more active role in the vindication of Jerusalem (v. 6). Jerusalem, however, will remain "on its own site" (v. 6b).

The next two oracles have a grammatical change to the third person, that is, the prophet speaks of the Lord (vv. 7-8). The Lord's preference for Judah is indicated by saving her "tents . . . first" (v. 7a) in order to prevent the exaltation of the "glory of the house of David and . . . inhabitants of Jerusalem" (v. 7b). It is unclear whether the references to Jerusalem mean that the community also needs purification or that the verse describes the humbled condition of the community in an ironic manner. Either interpretation provides the context for the next verse as well.

The Lord's protective care as "shield" will protect the Jerusalemites (v. 8). The verse recalls the prestigious memory of David, whom supplicants addressed as an "angel of God" (see 1 Sam 29:10; 2 Sam 14:17, 20; 19:28). Was David's line still represented in the community? Were there new hopes and dreams of a final age when David's ancestor would reign? The difficulty of dating the oracle prevents a response.

The final oracle (v. 9) is God's proclamation about the enemies of Jerusalem. It is a summary of the section.

12:10–13:1 Mourning in Jerusalem. The abrupt departure from the scene of the liberation of Jerusalem (12:1-9) to that of murder and mourning prompted some editions of the Bible to transpose the section to the end of 11:4-17. Nonetheless, the context of the previous passage (12:1-9) prepares for this section with its challenge for repentance. Verse 10, especially difficult to interpret, appears in Johannine literature (John 19:37; Rev 1:7), in Handel's *Messiah,* and in Christian devotion to the crucified Jesus.

tants of Jerusalem a spirit of grace and petition; and they shall look on him whom they have thrust through, and they shall mourn for him as one mourns for an only son, and they shall grieve over him as one grieves over a firstborn.

[11]On that day the mourning in Jerusalem shall be as great as the mourning of Hadadrimmon in the plain of Megiddo. [12]And the land shall mourn, each family apart: the family of the house of David, and their wives; the family of the house

Verse 10a promises God's gift, "a spirit of grace and petition," to the "house of David and . . . the inhabitants of Jerusalem." In addition to military victory (vv. 2-4; 6-9) and recognition of God's strength (v. 5), the community will participate in an interior renewal of heart (compare Ezek 36:26-27; 39:29; Joel 3:1-2 [2:28-29]). The "grace" of repentance appears to be the focus of the conversion. It is linked to a specific event: "They shall look on him whom they have thrust through." Intensive and extensive mourning follow (vv. 10b-14).

Who has been "pierced" (RSV)? Hebrew and Greek manuscripts differ here. Some read "on him," some read "on me." The more difficult reading ("on me") is preferred. The emendation "on him" denies the possibility that it is God who is pierced. Some commentators also question the translation "thrust through." Is it literal? Metaphorical? (see Lam 4:9; Prov 12:18). The same question arises when comparing verse 10 to Isa 53:5, which parallels the verse exactly.

Most commentators propose a literal interpretation for "piercing." The identity of the pierced one varies. Possibilities include a representative of God; a collectivity, such as the martyrs of Judah in the Maccabean era; a historical figure who had been murdered, for example, Josiah, Onias III, or Simon Maccabeus; a charismatic figure cast out by officials; the good shepherd of Zech 11. The identity remains unclear. The only "facts" from the verse are of a man murdered by the inhabitants of Jerusalem. Mourning and repentance occur afterward.

Verse 10b begins the detailed description of the mourning. The loss is especially poignant. The description recalls the Egyptians grieving over their first-born (Exod 4:22) and David's lament over his first-born (2 Sam 12:15-23) and over Absalom (2 Sam 18:33).

Two images note the intensity of grieving (v. 11). The name Hadadrimmon recalls the lamentation rites associated with the fall and spring seasons ritualized by the pagan weather-gods Hadad and Rimmon. Megiddo recalls the historical site at which the beloved King Josiah was killed (609 B.C.E.). National rites of mourning were conducted yearly (see 2 Chr 35:24-25).

The "land" and all its peoples are involved in mourning. First, royal houses are mentioned (v. 12; see 2 Sam 5:14), then priestly houses (v. 13; see Num

of Nathan, and their wives; [13]the family of the house of Levi, and their wives; the family of Shemei, and their wives; [14]and all the rest of the families, each family apart, and the wives apart.

13 **The End of Falsehood.** [1]On that day there shall be open to the house of David and to the inhabitants of Jerusalem, a fountain to purify from sin and uncleanness. [2]On that day, says the LORD of hosts, I will destroy the names of the idols from the land, so that they shall be mentioned no more; I will also take away the prophets and the spirit of uncleanness from the land. [3]If a man still prophesies, his parents, father and mother, shall say to him, "You shall not live, because you have spoken a lie in the name of the LORD." When he prophesies, his parents, father and mother, shall thrust him through.

[4]On that day, every prophet shall be ashamed to prophesy his vision, neither shall he assume the hairy mantle to mislead, [5]but he shall say, "I am no prophet, I am a tiller of the soil, for I have owned

3:18), then everyone else (v. 14). The phrase "and their wives" (5 times) suggests the separation of women and men during mourning.

Mourning "on that day" is connected with the opportunity "on that day" for purification "from sin and uncleanness" (13:1), which include all human misconduct, ritual and sexual impurity. There was a ritual cleansing for Zerubbabel and the community (see Zech 3:4; 9) and a similar promise according to Ezekiel (see Ezek 36:25).

In Isa 53:5 the piercing and death of God's messenger are related to forgiveness of sin. Yet in 13:1 Zechariah does not identify the pierced one as "servant." The identity of the fountain, its relationship to the one "thrust through," and the effect on the community are perplexing. The interpretation is difficult for us because Christian tradition has appropriated 12:10 and 13:1 to refer to Jesus.

13:2-6 Purification in Jerusalem. As Jerusalem would be cleansed of bogus leaders (see the commentary on 11:4-17), so idol worship and false prophets would be purged from the land. Ezekiel had specified that rejection of idolatry was part of the purification of the community (see Ezek 36). Some suggest that even worship of the temple may have been a problem.

Idol worship may have been promoted by dishonest prophets who sought to reclaim the glory of the preexilic era for themselves. The "spirit of uncleanness" associated with them impeded the community's relationship with God. The phrase occurs only here in the Old Testament, while it occurs frequently in the Gospels as something over which Jesus had power.

The punishment accorded to false prophets is described in verses 3-6. Parental accusation initiates the process (v. 3a; compare Deut 13:1-9; 18:19-22). If the son continued to prophesy, the parents were to "thrust him through" (v. 3b). The verb is the same used in 12:10.

Verse 4 suggests that the false prophet is somewhat honest by being ashamed to speak about visions or to assume a "hairy mantle" for leader-

land since my youth." ⁶And if anyone asks him, "What are these wounds on your chest?" he shall answer, "With these I was wounded in the house of my dear ones."

The Song of the Sword

⁷Awake, O sword, against my shepherd,
against the man who is my associate,
says the LORD of hosts.
Strike the shepherd
that the sheep may be dispersed,
and I will turn my hand against the
little ones.

⁸In all the land, says the LORD,
two thirds of them shall be cut off and
perish,
and one third shall be left.
⁹I will bring the one third through fire,
and I will refine them as silver is refined,
and I will test them as gold is tested.
They shall call upon my name, and
I will hear them.
I will say, "They are my people,"
and they shall say, "The LORD is my
God."

ship (see 2 Kgs 1:8). The irony of verse 5, however, contradicts this. There the false prophet mimics Amos, who preferred to till the soil (see Amos 7:14).

The deception is uncovered in verse 6, where the false prophet explains that his wounds are the result of punishment by his parents (v. 4b). Several suggest, however, that the lacerations were part of a ritual enacted for idols (see 1 Kgs 18:28), and the "dear ones" (RSV: "friends") were associates in the idolatrous worship (see Hos 2:7, 10-12; Ezek 23:5-9).

13:7-9 Sword and fire. The poetic section takes up the theme of shepherd and sheep. In contrast to previous sections (10:3; 11:4-17), where the shepherds were guilty of not fulfilling their duties, this shepherd is not condemned. He is described as the one who "is my associate" (v. 7a). The Hebrew word is otherwise limited to Leviticus, where regulations are given about relationships among the Israelites. "Near neighbor" is the translation there (see Lev 6:2; 18:20).

Who is this shepherd? As is the case with the pierced one, there are several interpretations. Some link the shepherd with the one who appeared before (see 11:4, 17; 12:10). Others suggest a good leader not previously mentioned. However uncertain the identification, the text describes the shepherd as the one against whom the sword is raised (13:7). Consequently, the sheep scatter and God turns a hand "against the little ones." Why the shepherd is struck down is not clear. The act precipitates the dispersal of the Lord's community, that is, the sheep.

The consequences are quite extreme. Two thirds "shall be cut off and perish" (v. 8a; compare Ezek 5:1-12). The remaining one third will be judged again. Traditional metaphors for God's cleansing action describe their plight: "into the fire" (compare 3:2; Ezek 5:4; Mal 3:3); refined "as silver is refined"; tested "as gold is tested" (v. 9b). The result is a reconciled relationship: "They shall call upon my name, and I will hear them . . . They are my people . . . The Lord is my God" (v. 9c).

14 The Fight for Jerusalem.

¹Lo, a day shall come for the LORD when the spoils shall be divided in your midst. ²And I will gather all the nations against Jerusalem for battle: the city shall be taken, houses plundered, women ravished; half of the city shall go into exile, but the rest of the people shall not be removed from the city. ³Then the LORD shall go forth and fight against those nations, fighting as on a day of battle. ⁴That day his feet shall rest upon the Mount of Olives, which is opposite Jerusalem to the east. The Mount of Olives shall be cleft in two from east to west by a very deep valley, and half of the mountain shall move to the north and half of it to the south. ⁵And the valley of the LORD's mountain shall be filled up when the valley of those two mountains reaches its edge; it shall be filled up as it was filled up by the earthquake in the days of King Uzziah of Judah. Then the LORD, my God, shall come, and all his holy ones with him.

⁶On that day there shall no longer be cold or frost. ⁷There shall be one continuous day, known to the LORD, not day and night, for in the evening time there shall be light.

⁸On that day, living waters shall flow from Jerusalem, half to the eastern sea, and half to the western sea, and it shall be so in summer and in winter. ⁹The LORD shall become king over the whole earth; on that day the LORD shall be the only one, and his name the only one.

¹⁰And from Geba to Rimmon in the Negeb, all the land shall turn into a plain; but Jerusalem shall remain exalted in its place. From the Gate of Benjamin to the place of the First Gate, to the Corner

14:1 Superscription. The ominous note that begins the final chapter of Zechariah parallels the "day of the Lord" (see Joel 1:15; 2:1). Two battles are then described in which the Lord will be present as antagonist against and protagonist for Jerusalem (vv. 2-3).

14:2-5 War and victory. In a first-person oracle God announces plans for "gathering all the nations against Jerusalem" (v. 2a). Grim consequences mark the defeat of the city: capture, plundered houses, ravished women, and half the inhabitants sent into exile (v. 2b). The rest of the people will remain in the city (compare Isa 1:9).

A grammatical change to the third person narrates another battle in which the Lord will fight against the nations (v. 3; compare Isa 43:13). Verses 4-5 contain the only mention of the Mount of Olives in the Old Testament (compare 2 Sam 15:30), while the earthquake is compared to the one attributed to Uzziah's seizure of priestly functions (see 2 Chr 26:16-21). No Davidic figure is mentioned; God's presence is primary.

14:6-11 Transformation of the land. The changes in the land noted in verses 4-5 continue in this section. Vegetation, animals, and persons alike will benefit from the favorable conditions (v. 7; compare Rev 21:23, 25).

According to verse 8, the valuable gift of water will be assured (compare Ezek 47:1-2; John 4:18; 7:37-39). The changes in the cosmos are related to the Lord's kingship "over the whole earth" (see Ps 97:1). It will be recognized and proclaimed in credal formula (v. 9; compare Deut 6:4-5).

Gate; and from the Tower of Hananel to the king's wine presses, ¹¹they shall occupy her. Never again shall she be doomed; Jerusalem shall abide in security.

¹²And this shall be the plague with which the LORD shall strike all the nations that have fought against Jerusalem: their flesh shall rot while they stand upon their feet, and their eyes shall rot in their sockets, and their tongues shall rot in their mouths.

¹³On that day there shall be among them a great tumult from the LORD: every man shall seize the hand of his neighbor, and the hand of each shall be raised against that of his neighbor. ¹⁴Judah also shall fight against Jerusalem. The riches of all the surrounding nations shall be gathered together, gold, silver, and garments, in great abundance.

¹⁵Similar to this plague shall be the plague upon the horses, mules, camels, asses, and upon all the beasts that are in those camps.

¹⁶All who are left of all the nations that came against Jerusalem shall come up year after year to worship the King, the LORD of hosts, and to celebrate the feast of Booths. ¹⁷If any of the families of the earth does not come up to Jerusalem to worship the King, the LORD of hosts, no rain shall fall upon them. ¹⁸And if the family of Egypt does not come up, or enter, upon them shall fall the plague which the LORD will inflict upon all the nations that do not come up to celebrate the feast of Booths. ¹⁹This shall be the punishment of Egypt, and the punishment of all the nations that do not come up to celebrate the feast of Booths.

Jerusalem will be accorded greater prominence (v. 10a). The territory described is from the reign of Josiah, who ruled twenty years before the Exile. Geba is six miles north of Jerusalem, and Rimmon is thirty-five miles southwest of Jerusalem (see 2 Kgs 23:8). Jerusalem, however, "shall remain exalted in its place" (v. 10b). Unfortunately, the places for the area markers of the city (v. 10c) are difficult to locate. Today they indicate four directions.

14:12-15 Plague and tumult. This section is an addition that enlarges upon the description of verse 3. The style is exaggerated, characteristic of apocalyptic writing. Verse 12 describes how the plague will affect "flesh," "eyes," and "tongue" (compare Ezek 28:21-22; 39:17-20; Rev 16:6; 19:17-18). Verse 13 attributes the "great tumult" among neighbors to the Lord. "Judah also shall fight against Jerusalem" (v. 14) ought to be interpreted as "with" or "in" Jerusalem, which the Hebrew also allows. Verse 15 concludes the section by mentioning a similar plague that will affect all the animals.

14:16-21 Celebration in Jerusalem. The final section of Second Zechariah parallels the corresponding section in First Zechariah (8:20-23). The verses indicate that nations that were Jerusalem's enemies will come to worship and celebrate the feast of Booths (v. 16). A curse will be leveled against "any of the families of the earth" who do not come for worship. "Lack of rainfall" will be the punishment (compare v. 8). The feast of Booths occurred just before the autumn rains.

Because of the Nile River, rain shortage will not be a serious problem for the Egyptians who fail to come to Jerusalem. However, the plague is the

²⁰On that day there shall be upon the bells of the horses, "Holy to the LORD." The pots in the house of the LORD shall be as the libation bowls before the altar. ²¹And every pot in Jerusalem and in Judah shall be holy to the LORD of hosts; and all who come to sacrifice shall take them and cook in them. On that day there shall no longer be any merchant in the house of the LORD of hosts.

potential curse for them and for all the nations that fail to celebrate the feast of Booths (vv. 18-19).

The concluding verses suggest the total dedication of Jerusalem and Judah to God. The temple itself is not the source of holiness. Instead, ordinary objects will become holy because of the persons who own them.

The Book of Zechariah has no conclusion. The editor probably wanted to use Malachi as the final message. For this purpose, the beginning of Malachi parallels Part One and Part Two of Second Zechariah (see p. 90).

Conclusion

The two parts of Second Zechariah develop the future judgment of God upon the temple-community and upon the nations. Chapters 9–11 outline battles against the enemy, consolation of the community, and the concept of shepherd and sheep. Chapters 12–14 use proto-apocalyptic language and content to dramatize what mourning and celebration entail. The second part also broadens the concept of the significance of Jerusalem and Judah for the nations.

Are there points of continuity between First Zechariah and Second Zechariah? The editor of the scroll and the persons responsible for the canonical status of Zechariah used literary devices to ensure that all fourteen chapters would be considered as *one* Minor Prophet (see pp. 59, 90).

Beyond literary considerations, there are religious relationships of continuity and development between the chapters.

a) Historically, First and Second Zechariah addressed communities separated by nearly two hundred years. While the political situation was different in the Persian and the Greek empires, the religious struggles were similar. Who will provide civic and religious leadership? What is required? Can an emperor fulfill expectations?

b) In proclaiming a future in which God would initiate victory, both communities heard about their renewed relationship to God. God as warrior and protective presence would give them comfort and support for their activities. Before this happened, however, the community would suffer the ravages of war and the comprehensive process of purification.

c) Fidelity to God's covenant through faithful living and restored worship would characterize those who lived in Judah. Evil is not denied but recognized. God assured the communities that evil will not be ultimately victorious. Transgressors could repent or be punished.

d) God's relationship to the nations, as well as their own relationship to traditional enemies, was developed in radically new perspectives. "On that day" Israel and the nations would share in God's compassion. They would live together in a land free from war and for holiness. Communal worship would be one symbol of the new reality.

e) The vision of an unexpected future was offered to both communities while the uncertainties of the present weighed heavily in their daily experience. How would the communities prepare for the blessings of "that day"? Attention to God's word spoken in the past and reinterpreted by the minor prophet Zechariah would provide some direction in living during periods of "in betweenness."

The Book of Malachi

Introduction

Authorship

What is known about the author of the Book of Malachi is derived from 3:1, where the phrase "my messenger" occurs. An editor probably used the Hebrew transliteration (*mal'achi*) "Malachi" for 1:1, where the proper name appears. The name Malachi does not occur anywhere else in the Old Testament. The absence of any precise chronology and genealogy in the superscription (1:1) lends support to the suggestion that the author was an anonymous prophet.

The superscription includes the word "oracle" (the Hebrew means "burden") rather than a personal name. It parallels Zech 9:1; 12:1, where the literary device marks collections of oracles that were added to First Zechariah (see p. 90). While a common superscription unites Second Zechariah and Malachi, the historical background, literary structures, and religious significance of the collected oracles differ greatly.

Dating of the text

According to its canonical position, the Book of Malachi is the twelfth of the Minor Prophets. This location is not conclusive for establishing a chronology of the text. The Book of Malachi describes situations that place the prophet about fifty years after the completion of the temple (515 B.C.E.) and just before the ministry of Ezra (about 460–445 B.C.E.). For an understanding of the historical context, see p. 9.

The book offers some perspective about the challenges the prophet encountered. Although the community was under the office of a governor (see 1:8; Hag 1:1; Neh 5:14), civic authority had declined. The priests had assumed civic and religious authority for the community. The priests, however, were irresponsible leaders, failing to correct several abuses: worship, moral and social problems, and mixed marriages.

The book offers valuable insights into Jewish communities in the mid-fifth century B.C.E. It corresponds to Ezra and Nehemiah and supplements these books. It is a historical witness to how a community may participate in the process of restoration with a population of about twenty thousand living in an area twenty by twenty-five miles square.

Composition of the text

A collection of oracles has been edited and unified by a literary device called the disputation. It is a catechetical structure consisting of three elements: (a) an affirmation of God or the prophet occurs at the beginning of each section; (b) a question arises from the audience, usually a reproach or a complaint; (c) God or the prophet responds often with an argument.

The prophet and the editor depend on Ezekiel and Deuteronomy for ideas and images for the disputation. The Levitical sermons of the Chronicler are similar in structure and content. The two appendices were added to conclude the Book of Malachi and the scroll of the Twelve Minor Prophets. The identification of the precursor of the messianic day links the collection to the New Testament (see the commentary on 3:23-24).

Outline of the book

Like Joel and First Zechariah, where the numbering of chapters and verses are different, the Book of Malachi has one discrepancy in the numbering. This commentary, based on the New American Bible, follows the Hebrew text, while other Bibles and commentaries may use the Greek text. The chart compares the versions.

Hebrew Text	Greek Text
3:19-24	4:1-6

In this commentary the numbering of the Greek text is in brackets.

PART ONE:	Oracles (1:2–3:21 [1:2–4:3])
1:1	Superscription
1:2-5	First Oracle: God's Love for Israel
1:6–2:9	Second Oracle: Sins of the Priests
2:10-16	Third Oracle: Sins of the Community
2:17–3:5	Fourth Oracle: God's Justice
3:6-12	Fifth Oracle: Ritual Offenses
3:13-21 [3:13–4:3]	Sixth Oracle: God's Servants
PART TWO:	Appendices (3:22-24 [4:4-6])
3:22 [4:4]	Conclusion of Twelve Minor Prophets
3:23-24 [4:5-6]	Identification of Precursor

The Book of Malach

Text and Commentary

1 ¹An oracle. The word of the LORD to Israel through Malachi.

Israel Preferred to Edom

²I have loved you, says the LORD;
but you say, "How have you loved us?"

³Was not Esau Jacob's brother? says the LORD:
yet I loved Jacob, but hated Esau;
I made his mountains a waste,
his heritage a desert for jackals.
⁴If Edom says, "We have been crushed
but we will rebuild the ruins,"

PART ONE: ORACLES

Mal 1:2–3:21 [1:2–4:3]

The six sections of Part One are addressed exclusively to Israel and concern its covenant relationship with God. A covenant theme is developed in the first oracle, which proclaims God's love for Israel (1:2-5). It forms an inclusion with the first appendix, where the people are enjoined to "remember the laws of Moses . . . the statutes and ordinances for all Israel" (3:22 [4:4]). Abuses within the community are discussed in connection with covenant stipulations.

1:1 Superscription. For discussion of "an oracle" and "Malachi," see above (p. 108). "Israel" refers to the whole nation, not merely the northern kingdom. The phrase introduces the focus of Part One: concern for the Jewish community and the experiences of daily life. There is no discussion about the role of the nations; neither are there any judgments of future orientation.

1:2-5 First oracle: God's love for Israel. The catechetical pattern, the structure for the oracles, uses language suggestive of an intimate relationship between the dialogue partners. The oracle begins with a statement of the Lord: "I have loved you" (v. 2a). Anticipating the listeners' response, the Lord's oracle continues: "but you say, 'How have you loved us?'" (v. 2b).

The disputation concludes with a response from the Lord (vv. 3-5). The Edomite situation is offered as a vivid memory from tradition. The mutual distrust of two brothers (Esau and Jacob) ignited enmity between their families and descendants, an enmity that grew to an irreconcilable impasse when Babylon invaded Jerusalem (586 B.C.E.). Complicity *with* the enemy and *against* Judah was unforgivable to the exiles and their descendants (for the

Thus says the Lord of hosts:
They indeed may build, but I will tear down,
And they shall be called the land of guilt,
the people with whom the Lord is angry forever.

⁵Your own eyes shall see it, and you will say,
"Great is the Lord, even beyond the land of Israel."

Sins of the Priests and Levites

⁶A son honors his father,

historical development of the tradition, see pp. 33–34 and the commentary on Obad 10-14, p. 38).

In verse 3a God asks a rhetorical question to situate the response: "Was not Esau Jacob's brother?" Next, the declaration of God's love identifies Jacob as the special one (v. 3b). The Hebrew verb designates the *elective* sense of "love." The specific meaning was used in the covenantal context when God declared love for Israel (see Deut 4:37; 7:7, 8; 10:15) and extended an invitation to Israel to respond in love (see Deut 5:10; 6:5; 11:1, 13).

The choice of Jacob ought to be seen as an election. This is not clear in the English translation. The election of Jacob rather than Esau does not entail "hatred" toward Esau. It is a matter of choice, of the mysterious decision of God. Ironically, although Jacob was chosen, his family experienced the Exile while Esau's did not. Paul uses verses 2-3 to develop the theme of election and predestination in Rom 9:13. In the present context, however, predestination is not the issue.

Another appeal to the community's experience is remembrance of the fate of Edom after the Exile. The Lord ravaged the area, toppling the mountains (where the tribe lived in safety) and ruining the land (v. 3c). Historically, the event corresponds to the raids of Arabian tribes that greatly diminished Edom's influence in the Negeb about a century after the fall of Jerusalem.

The downfall of Edom appears to be permanent. Even if they attempt "to rebuild the ruins . . . I will tear down" (v. 4a). More devastating than the ruined land is the name that Edom will bear forever: "wicked country" (RSV) and the judgment of the Lord: "the people with whom the Lord is angry forever" (v. 4b).

The oracle concludes with a third appeal to experience (v. 5a). The conviction of being chosen by the faithful God will impel the community to praise (v. 5b; compare Zech 9:1-8). The ironic expectation of the prophet is a hope that the community will become observant; look beyond Israel and acknowledge that God's dominion is greater than the "land of Israel."

1:6–2:9 Second oracle: Sins of the priests. Eight oracles have been combined to disclose the two principal sins of the priests: offering polluted sacrifices (1:6-14) and abrogating the roles of teacher and leader (2:1-9). Each oracle is identified by an introductory or concluding prophetic formula: "says

and a servant fears his master;
If then I am a father,
 where is the honor due to me?
And if I am a master,
 where is the reverence due to me?—
So says the LORD of hosts to you, O
 priests,
 who despise his name.
But you ask, "How have we despised
 your name?"
7 By offering polluted food on my altar!

Then you ask, "How have we polluted
 it?"
 By saying the table of the LORD may
 be slighted!
8When you offer a blind animal for sacrifice,
 is this not evil?
When you offer the lame or the sick,
 is it not evil?
Present it to your governor; see if he
 will accept it,

the Lord of hosts." The literary structure continues the disputation format. The characteristic elements indicate expansions.

The sin of offering polluted sacrifices is described in two sections (vv. 6-9; 10-14). The first section begins with a comparison of familial and house-hold relationships with covenant relationship (v. 6a). The Lord questions the fidelity of the covenant partners. The tone of the rhetorical questions suggests that the covenant relationship has deteriorated: "Where is the honor due to me? Where is the reverence due to me?" (v. 6b; compare Exod 4:22; Hos 11:1; Isa 1:2).

The prophetic formula follows (v. 6b). What is unusual here is the addi-tion "to you, O priests, who despise his name." The grammatical change from the third person to the second person suggests that the judgment is that of the prophet who has spoken the Lord's word or of an editor. The charge of despising the Lord's name is extremely serious. It is equivalent to despis-ing the very being of God.

The next two topics are concerned with priestly matters (vv. 6c-7: see v. 12). There were very strict standards for suitable sacrificial offerings (see Lev 22:18-25; Deut 15:21; 17:1). Contemporary sociological criticism of bib-lical texts confirms the complexity of standards in regard to purity (holiness) and pollution (sinfulness).

The phrase "table of the Lord" appears only here in the Old Testament, although the idea appears elsewhere (see Ps 23:5; Ezek 44:16). The tables for slaughtering the sacrifices were located at the gates of the inner court of the temple. A single table was located in the sanctuary, where only the priest was allowed (see Ezek 40:39-43).

The questions about sacrifice are answered by additional rhetorical ques-tions of the Lord appealing to priestly experiences (v. 8; see vv. 3-5). Blind, lame, and sick animals constitute "polluted food" (v. 8a). Such offerings would not be acceptable to the governor nor invite his hospitality (v. 8b). The governor's refusal and attitude are the analogy for God's disposition.

or welcome you, says the LORD of
hosts.
⁹So now if you implore God for mercy
on us,
when you have done the like
Will he welcome any of you?
says the LORD of hosts.
¹⁰Oh, that one among you would shut the
temple gates
to keep you from kindling fire on my
altar in vain!
I have no pleasure in you, says the LORD
of hosts;
neither will I accept any sacrifice from
your hands,
¹¹For from the rising of the sun, even to its
setting,
my name is great among the nations;
And everywhere they bring sacrifice to
my name,
and a pure offering;
For great is my name among the nations,
says the LORD of hosts.
¹²But you behave profanely toward me by
thinking
the LORD's table and its offering may
be polluted,
and its food slighted.
¹³You also say, "What a burden!"
and you scorn it, says the LORD of
hosts;
You bring in what you seize, or the
lame, or the sick;

An ironic question from the prophet concludes the oracle (v. 9; compare Zech
7:2).

The Lord's response to the polluted offerings is developed in the second
section (vv. 10-14). Let there be a cessation of all temple sacrifice (v. 10a;
see Ezek 40:39-41). God's preference is for *no* sacrifice: "I take no pleasure
in you . . . neither will I accept any sacrifice from your hands" (v. 10b).
The statement would cause anxiety among the priests. Their function as well
as the efforts of the community to restore the temple for worship were being
threatened.

The Lord's response continues a contrast between the priests and people
of the covenant community and the "nations." There are various interpretations of verse 11. Some commentators suggest that the verse describes imminent expectations of a messianic age when Gentiles will worship with Jews
(compare Isa 66:18-21; Zech 14:21). A few Catholic commentators propose
that the verse is a reference to the sacrifice of the Mass. Others relate the
verse to the situation of the Diaspora Jews and their synagogue activities
(prayer and study), which have replaced or substituted for temple sacrifice.
The last argument is most probable. However, whatever the particular interpretation may be, the general context identifies a type of activity that is
pleasing to God.

The remaining verses of the section continue the contrast between the
priests and the nations by indicting priestly thoughts and behavior.

The concluding oracle of the section issues a curse to the priest who de-
ceives himself and the community by offering a "gelding" and holding back
a "male" animal (v. 14a; see Lev 22:18). There is an implied contrast between

113

yes, you bring it as a sacrifice.
Shall I accept it from your hands?
says the LORD.
[14] Cursed is the deceiver, who has in his
flock a male,
but under his vow sacrifices to the
LORD a gelding;
For a great King am I, says the LORD of
hosts,
and my name will be feared among
the nations.

2 [1] And now, O priests, this commandment is for you:
If you do not listen,
[2] And if you do not lay it to heart,
to give glory to my name, says the
LORD of hosts,

I will send a curse upon you
and of your blessing I will make a
curse.
Yes, I have already cursed it,
because you do not lay it to heart.
[3] Lo, I will deprive you of the shoulder
and I will strew dung in your faces,
The dung of your feasts,
and you will be carried off with it.
[4] Then you will know that I sent you this
commandment
because I have a covenant with Levi,
says the LORD of hosts.
[5] My covenant with him was one of life
and peace;
fear I put in him, and he feared me,
and stood in awe of my name.

the covenant community and the "nations." The Lord is a "great King whose name will be feared among the nations" (v. 14b). The repetition of "great" (vv. 5, 11, 14) and "name" (vv. 6, 11, 14) throughout the indictment for polluted sacrifices (vv. 6-14) emphasizes the nature of God and how inadequately the priests respond.

The second indictment condemns the failure of the priests as teachers and leaders because they have abandoned personal integrity (2:1-9). The entire section is the Lord's response in covenantal terminology. The priests will be cursed if they do not heed the Lord's warning (vv. 1-2; see Deut 27:14–28:68). "Shoulder" (v. 3) is interpreted literally as the choice portion of animal sacrifices given to the priests (see Deut 18:3). The Revised Standard Version renders "shoulder" as "offspring," implying that the whole priestly lineage will be cut off with no successors, while the New English Bible translates the term as "arm," suggesting that priests will be prevented from officiating at the altar.

God offers a sign to the priests that the commandment is intended for them. It is the "covenant with Levi," whereby "life and peace" were offered. Levi responded by fearing God and standing in awe of God's name (vv. 4-5). In addition, Levi spoke true doctrine (*torah*) honestly, lived "in integrity and uprightness, and turned many away from evil" (v. 6; compare Deut 31:9-13). While the covenant with Levi (v. 4) is not recorded in the Old Testament, it is presupposed in other texts (see Jer 33:21; compare Num 25:11-13).

The covenant with Levi is the model for the priest, who is to be knowledgeable in the law and is to instruct the community (v. 7a; see Deut 17:9; 33:10). The priest must be faithful to the covenant "because he is the

⁶True doctrine was in his mouth,
and no dishonesty was found upon
his lips;
He walked with me in integrity and uprightness,
and turned many away from evil.
⁷For the lips of the priest are to keep
knowledge,
and instruction is to be sought from
his mouth,
because he is the messenger of the
Lord of hosts.
⁸But you have turned aside from the
way,
and have caused many to falter by

your instruction;
You have made void the covenant of
Levi,
says the Lord of hosts.
⁹I, therefore, have made you contemptible
and base before all the people,
Since you do not keep my ways,
but show partiality in your decisions.

Sins of the People

¹⁰Have we not all the one Father?
Has not the one God created us?
Why then do we break faith with each
other,

messenger of the Lord of hosts" (v. 7b). This is the one verse in the Old Testament where a priest is given the title "messenger," which traditionally was
associated with a prophet. The transfer of title and function from prophet
to priest may refer to the historical circumstances of Malachi's experience.

The comprehensive model of the covenant with Levi and the additional
role of "messenger of the Lord of hosts" are the basis for the judgment of
the priests (vv. 8-9). They have not been faithful to the obligations of the
covenant nor to their role as teachers and leaders (v. 8). Since they voided
the covenant of Levi, the Lord has stripped them of their status. They have
become "contemptible and base before all the people," since they refuse to
keep God's covenant and to instruct the community in its stipulations (v. 9).

Some commentators have suggested that the description of the covenant
with Levi and its authority may be a reference to the contrast between the
Zadokite priests (returnees from Babylon) and the Levites. The latter had
been given menial tasks in the service of the temple, while the priests were
important functionaries (see pp. 10–11). Malachi may be favoring Levitical
rather than Zadokite jurisdiction in the community.

2:10-16 Sins of the community. The community is guilty of breaking
covenant with God in different situations. While the section begins with a
general admonition (v. 10), the sin that is emphasized is the faithlessness of
husbands to wives. Divorce, which Jewish law only permitted husbands to
initiate under specific conditions, was becoming troublesome (see Deut 24:1-4;
Hos 2:4; compare Ezra 9–10).

The returned exiles were wealthy and may have expected to enhance their
position in the community by marrying a local woman. The practice of
divorce meant that the community included many single, divorced Jewish
women. Intermarriage meant that non-Jewish mothers would be responsible

violating the covenant of our fathers?
[11]Judah has broken faith; an abominable thing
has been done in Israel and in Jerusalem.
Judah has profaned the temple which the LORD loves,
and has married an idolatrous woman.
[12]May the LORD cut off from the man who does this
both witness and advocate out of the tents of Jacob,
and anyone to offer sacrifice to the LORD of hosts!
[13]This also you do: the altar of the LORD you cover
with tears, weeping and groaning,
Because he no longer regards your sacrifice
nor accepts it favorably from your hand;

for teaching their children the practices of a religion that was foreign to them. It is not clear from the text what reasons were given for the divorce proceedings.

The prophetic injunction goes beyond earlier Jewish law, which regarded the wife as a possession of the husband (see Exod 20:17). The prophet identifies the relationship between husband and wife as a covenant that affects the partners, the individuals in their relationship to God, their children, and the other members of the community. As in the case of the indictments against the priests, here the covenant is the basis of the indictment against the community.

The prophet poses rhetorical questions that address the reality of the community's experience of common origin to begin a new disputation (v. 10a; compare Deut 32:6; Isa 63:16; 64:8). Referring to a common historical tradition, the prophet points out the "abomination" (RSV) that Judah, Jerusalem, and Israel have committed (v. 11a). "Abomination" is a technical term used to describe idols and the practice of idol worship forbidden by the covenant (see Deut 32:16; Isa 44:19). The present community is guilty of the same offense (v. 11b).

The consequences of the community's action (v. 11b) are interpreted in two ways. Literally, the verse identifies *worship* as unacceptable to the Lord due to the covenant faithlessness of the worshipers. Metaphorically, the "temple," "sanctuary" (RSV), "holiness" (NEB) of the Lord may also identify the *community members*, who are called to belong to God (see Deut 32:9). Whether worship or the members themselves are described, the indictment is the same: members have married "the daughter of a foreign god" (RSV; see 1 Kgs 11:1-8; Neh 13:23-27). Mixed marriages violate the covenant with God *and* the bond that unites the community (see Exod 34:13-16; Deut 7:1-4).

The first section concludes with a threatening curse (v. 12a). The identification of "witness and advocate" is difficult. Most commentators propose

¹⁴And you say, "Why is it?"—
　Because the Lᴏʀᴅ is witness
　between you and the wife of your
　　youth,
With whom you have broken faith
　though she is your companion, your
　　betrothed wife.
¹⁵Did he not make one being, with flesh
　and spirit:
　and what does that one require but
godly offspring?
You must then safeguard life that is your
　own,
　and not break faith with the wife of
　　your youth.
¹⁶For I hate divorce,
　says the Lᴏʀᴅ, the God of Israel,
And covering one's garment with in-
　justice,
　says the Lᴏʀᴅ of hosts;

a universal meaning, that is, anyone involved in the situation. Exclusion from the community and prohibition to sacrifice in the temple are the closely related civic and religious punishments (v. 12b).

Sacrifices are no longer acceptable (v. 13b; compare 1:10b). Verse 14a is the only occurrence of a community question in the disputation: "Why is it?" The relationship of faithful living to genuine ritual is reiterated for the community as it was for the priests (see the commentary on 1:6b-13; 2:3-9). The prophet responds to the question by identifying the Lord as "witness between you and the wife of your youth" (v. 14a; compare Isa 54:6; Prov 5:18).

The severity of the broken relationship is indicated in verses 15-16. This obscure text may be an addition by scribal editors who disagreed with the prophet's insight. The emphasis is on God who created each person as "one being, with flesh and spirit," who in turn creates "godly offspring." The implication is that according to the model of God who is one, the married partners ought to be faithful to their union as "one" and "not break faith" (v. 15). Synonymous parallelism (vv. 14b, 15b) underscores the importance of fidelity to the marriage covenant.

Verse 16 consists of two divine oracles, which conclude the section. Two situations are hateful to the Lord. The first is divorce. While the English translations concur about the clause "I hate divorce," the Hebrew renders it "if he hates send (her) away" (v. 16a). Perhaps the text was amended by a scribe who desired to bring Malachi's teaching into conformity with earlier permission for divorce (see Deut 24:1). The oracle is attributed to the "Lord, the God of Israel," a phrase used nowhere else in the Old Testament. The title fits the context of continuing covenant relationships.

"Covering one's garments with injustice" is the second object of the Lord's hatred (v. 16b). It is an obscure clause. The "garment" may be a symbol for the divorce partners. The final injunction of the prophet (v. 16c) forms an inclusion with verse 15b, which brackets the Lord's oracles. It is a general exhortation to be faithful in all relationships with others and with God.

You must then safeguard life that is your own,
and not break faith.

¹⁷You have wearied the LORD with your words,
yet you say, "How have we wearied him?"
By your saying, "Every evildoer
is good in the sight of the LORD,
And he is pleased with him";
or else, "Where is the just God?"

The Messenger of the Covenant

3 ¹Lo, I am sending my messenger
to prepare the way before me;

And suddenly there will come to the temple
the LORD whom you seek,
And the messenger of the covenant
whom you desire.
Yes, he is coming, says the LORD of hosts.
²But who will endure the day of his coming?
And who can stand when he appears?
For he is like the refiner's fire,
or like the fuller's lye.
³He will sit refining and purifying [silver],
and he will purify the sons of Levi,

2:17–3:5 Fourth oracle: God's justice. Consistent with the focus on Israel, God's justice will be enacted upon that community through a judgment that both eliminates social abuses and purifies the Levites. The section 3:1-21 [3:13–4:6] is characterized as "proto-apocalyptic" because of the imminent judgment of the Lord (see p. 15). Nonetheless, the "nations" are not included in the judgment (compare Joel 3–4 [2:28–3:21] and Second Zechariah).

The disputation begins with a statement from the prophet (2:17a; compare Isa 43:24), followed by a question formulated to anticipate the audience (2:17b). The response identifies two attitudes of the community that are weakening the covenantal relationship. The people assume that evil is pleasing in God's sight (see Jer 12:1; Hab 1:2-4). Their belief in a just God is waning, that is, they are beginning to doubt God's existence (2:17c).

Thus the final verse of chapter 2 provides a transition to the next theme, God's justice. The questions about "wearying God" and the "just God" are repeated (3:13-15) and answered (3:16-18) in the context of the sixth oracle (3:13-21 [3:13–4:3]).

The next section (3:1-5) offers an entirely new focus on the "messenger" who will appear before the Lord's judgment. Verses 1a and 5 are first-person oracles representing God, while verses 2-4 are a third-person narration of the prophet. God announces that "my messenger" will be sent to prepare "the way before me" (v. 1a), while the prophet proclaims the coming of this messenger (v. 1b).

The identity of the messenger of the covenant is unclear. Verses 1b-4 are confusing. Did the editor of the book identify "my messenger" with the prophet Malachi (see p. 108)? Will the "messenger of the covenant" fulfill a Levitical role (see 2:4-8; compare Isa 40:3)? Are "my messenger" and the "messenger of the covenant" different individuals or the same individual?

Refining them like gold or like silver
that they may offer due sacrifice to
the LORD.
⁴Then the sacrifice of Judah and Jerusalem
will please the LORD,
as in the days of old, as in years gone
by.
⁵I will draw near to you for judgment,
and I will be swift to bear witness
Against the sorcerers, adulterers, and
perjurers,

those who defraud the hired man of
his wages,
Against those who defraud widows and
orphans;
those who turn aside the stranger,
and those who do not fear me,
says the LORD of hosts.
⁶Surely I, the LORD, do not change,
nor do you cease to be sons of Jacob.
⁷Since the days of your fathers you have
turned aside

Does the description designate an angelic being? God? Or the imminent
presence of God?

The prophet probably envisioned "my messenger" as a Levitical figure.
A later editor, however, identified him as Elijah (see 3:23 [4:5]). It is possible that the Levitical figure could also function as the "messenger of the
covenant." While commentators are divided about the identity of the messengers in Malachi, the messenger is unanimously identified in the Gospel
traditions as John the Baptist (see Mark 1:2-8; Matt 3:1-11; Luke 3:2-16).

Verses 2-4 describe the coming of the Lord as judge in traditional
metaphorical language. The double questions about the coming of the Lord
refer to battle imagery (v. 2a; see 2 Kgs 10:4; Amos 2:15). "Like a refiner's
fire or like the fuller's lye" are consistent images in prophecy (see Isa 1:25;
Jer 6:29-30; Ezek 22:17-22). In Malachi the images signify that God will remove all impurities and cleanse the sons of Levi (vv. 2b-3; compare Zech
13:9).

In verse 4 the prophet compares future Levitical sacrifices on behalf of
Judah and Jerusalem with the sacrifices that pleased the Lord in the past.
The era of Moses is an appropriate identification for that period (see Jer 2:2;
Isa 63:9, 11; compare Amos 5:25; Jer 7:22). The purification and acceptance
of Levitical sacrifices (vv. 2-4) present a sharp contrast to the concluding
verse of the section, which enumerates the evildoers who will be judged
(v. 5; see 2:17c).

Verse 5a presents a court context in which the Lord is both witness and
judge (see 2:14). With the exception of sorcerers (see Deut 18:10-11; Jer 27:9),
all the groups responsible for social evils are indicted: adulterers and perjurers (compare 2:11-16); employers who defraud (see Lev 19:13; Deut
24:14-15); those who oppress widows and orphans (see Zech 7:10) or maltreat
the sojourner (v. 5b). The perpetrators of social evils are described as the
ones "who do not fear me" (v. 5c).

from my statutes, and have not kept
 them.
Return to me, and I will return to you,
 says the LORD of hosts.
Yet you say, "How must we return?"
⁸ Dare a man rob God? Yet you are
 robbing me!
And you say, "How do we rob you?"
 In tithes and in offerings!

⁹You are indeed accursed,
 for you, the whole nation, rob me.
¹⁰Bring the whole tithe
 into the storehouse,
That there may be food in my house,
 and try me in this, says the LORD of
 hosts:
Shall I not open for you the floodgates
 of heaven,

3:6-12 Fifth oracle: Ritual offenses. Four oracles of the Lord have been combined in the section to address the community about the quality of their ritual activity. Their deeds indict them when they approach the altar, just as the priestly activities and attitudes condemned the priests earlier (1:6–2:9).

The Lord's statement about the covenant bond initiates the disputation (v. 6; compare 1:2; 3:5; Gen 27:36). Next, there is a judgment about how that relationship was defiled throughout history (v. 7a). A plea to return to the Lord concludes the oracle (v. 7b). Malachi, like Zechariah, does not idealize past generations (see Zech 1:2, 4). Both invoke earlier Jewish tradition in pleading with their communities to return to God (see the commentary on Zech 1:3).

The Lord anticipates the question of the community: "How must we return?" (v. 7c) and responds with instructions about tithing. This is an unusual prophetic injunction, for earlier tradition insisted that community gifts were neither needed (see Ps 50:7-15) nor acceptable (see Amos 5:21-23; Isa 43:23).

Tithes represented one-tenth of an individual's produce; this portion was given to the Levites, who in turn gave a tithe to the priests (see Num 18:23-24, 28). According to the law, tithes were given to the Levites and to destitute members of the community every three years (see Deut 14:28-29). Therefore, if tithes were not given, members of the community suffered (compare 3:5). Offerings were portions of sacrifices and voluntary gifts given to the priests (see Exod 29:27-28; 25:2-7). By "robbing" God, the community is judged: "you are indeed accursed" (v. 9; compare Prov 11:24).

Three oracles describe blessings promised to the community if they return to God by obeying the law about tithes and offerings (vv. 10-12). This is probably the prophet's response to those members who doubted God's existence (see 2:17).

The imperative "try me in this" suggests God's willingness to be tested. God's fidelity to the community will be seen in the blessings they enjoy (v. 10b). However, an obedient response of the community is a pre-condition for God's blessings. Two images of land harvest describe some of God's bless-

to pour down blessing upon you without measure? ¹¹For your sake I will forbid the locust to destroy your crops; And the vine in the field will not be barren, says the LORD of hosts. ¹²Then all nations will call you blessed, for you will be a delightful land, says the LORD of hosts. ¹³You have defied me in word, says the LORD, yet you ask, "What have we spoken against you?"

¹⁴You have said, "It is vain to serve God, and what do we profit by keeping his command, And going about in penitential dress in awe of the LORD of hosts? ¹⁵Rather must we call the proud blessed; for indeed evildoers prosper, and even tempt God with impunity." ¹⁶Then they who fear the LORD spoke with one another, and the LORD listened attentively; And a record book was written before him of those who fear the LORD and trust

ings: no locusts will "destroy your crops; and the vine . . . will not be barren" (v. 11; compare Joel 1:4; Hag 2:16, 19; Zech 8:12).

Abundant harvests will be evident to the nations, which "will call you blessed, for you will be a delightful land" (v. 12). Unlike Zechariah, there is no indication here that the nations will share in God's blessings bestowed on the community (see Zech 14:16-19).

3:13-21 [3:13–4:3] Sixth oracle: God's servants. The priests had been indicted for their actions and words. The same judgment is passed on the community, who had already been indicted for their actions (3:6-12). This section describes why their words nullify the covenant with God. The first part contains the questions of the evildoers. The second part is a contrast between those who fear God and the evildoers.

The attitudes of the community indicate skepticism. Lack of personal gain in observing the covenant requirements contributes to an apathetic spirit. The description of being clothed "in penitential dress" (NAB), "as in mourning" (RSV), "behaving with deference" (NEB) is difficult to interpret. It may identify a particular group of the community, such as the Levites, who had suffered because the tithes were not sufficient. They dressed in repentance but continued to experience hardships (compare Neh 13:10-13). Not only is the community lacking in fervor, but judgment suffers as well (v. 15; compare 2:17; Ps 73:2-14). Although these attitudes are widespread among community members, the situation is not a definitive one.

A shift from the Lord's oracles to prophetic narration and oracles announces the second part of this section. Responding to the disputation (vv. 13-15), some members seek to "return" to God (v. 16; compare 2:1). To preserve a record of those who "fear the Lord and trust in his name," a "book of remembrance" is compiled (v. 16c; compare 2:4-5). The book is a traditional symbol in Jewish tradition (see Exod 32:32-33; Isa 4:3; Ps 69:29; com-

in his name.

¹⁷And they shall be mine, says the LORD of
hosts,
my own special possession, on the
day I take action.
And I will have compassion on them,
as a man has compassion on his son
who serves him.
¹⁸Then you will again see the distinction
between the just and the wicked;
Between him who serves God,
and him who does not serve him.
¹⁹For lo, the day is coming, blazing like an
oven,
when all the proud and all evildoers
will be stubble,
And the day that is coming will set them
on fire,
leaving them neither root nor branch,
says the LORD of hosts.
²⁰But for you who fear my name, there
will arise
the sun of justice with its healing rays;
And you will gambol like calves out of
the stall
²¹ and tread down the wicked;
They will become ashes under the soles
of your feet,
on the day I take action, says the
LORD of hosts.

pare Esth 6:1-2). The phrase "book of remembrance," however, occurs only
in Malachi.

God promises the people another blessing. They will be "mine . . . my
own special possession," thus reaffirming the covenant with the Lord (v. 17a;
see Exod 19:5; Deut 14:2; Ps 135:4). Compassion is another blessing from
God (v. 17b; see 1:6a; 3:6). The ability to "again see the distinction between
the just and the wicked" (v. 18a; compare 2:17b) will definitively challenge:
"Every evildoer is good in the sight of the Lord" (v. 2:17c).

The second distinction that will become clear is between the one who
serves God and the one who does not serve God (v. 18b). The approaching
judgment of God will satisfy the scoffers' question: "Where is the just God?"
(2:17c). The apocalyptic image of judgment as fire describes the separation
of the community. Unlike the "refining" fire (3:2), the "blazing" quality will
reduce "all the proud and all evildoers" (to) "stubble . . . leaving them neither
root or branch" (v. 19 [4:1]).

For "you who fear my name, there will arise the sun of justice with its
healing rays" (v. 20a [4:2a]; compare 3:16c; Isa 57:18-19; Luke 1:78-79). This
is the one verse where the "sun of righteousness" (RSV) occurs in the Old
Testament. Most commentators attribute the symbolism to the Egyptian and
Mesopotamian sun-god, who is pictured with a winged solar disc on many
Near Eastern monuments. The god functioned as judge among the gods of
the pantheon.

Experiencing the "sun of righteousness" will rouse the energies of those
who fear the Lord: "you shall break loose like calves released from the stall"
(v. 20b [4:2]; NEB) and "tread down the wicked" (v. 21a [4:3a]). Consistent
with the image of consuming fire (v. 19), the wicked will "become ashes under
the soles of your feet on the day I take action" (v. 21b [4:3b]). God will vin-

²²Remember the law of Moses my servant,
which I enjoined upon him on Horeb,
The statutes and ordinances
for all Israel.
²³Lo, I will send you
Elijah, the prophet,
Before the day of the LORD comes,

the great and terrible day,
²⁴To turn the hearts of the fathers to their
children,
and the hearts of the children to their
fathers,
Lest I come and strike
the land with doom.

dicate those who fear the Lord (see Deut 32:35; Prov 20:22). The clause "on
the day I take action" (vv. 17b; 23b [4:3b]) is an inclusion bracketing the
Lord's future activities.

PART TWO: APPENDICES

Mal 3:22-24 [4:4-6]

The appendices summarize characteristic teaching, identify the messenger
of the Lord, and describe the day of the Lord. There is no consensus about
when they were combined, edited, and added to Part One of Malachi. Their
inclusion indicates the importance of the closing verses of Malachi, the scroll
of the Twelve Minor Prophets, and the conclusion of the Old Testament for
future generations of communities.

"Remember the law of Moses . . . all Israel" (v. 22 [4:4]) points to the
importance of the first five books of the Old Testament. Each phrase of the
verse is an exhortation to be committed to Mosaic law. The phrases are taken
from Deuteronomy's covenantal descriptions.

The next verse identifies the mysterious messenger of Mal 3:1 as the
prophet Elijah (v. 23a [4:5a]). Descriptions of him in 2 Kings and Sirach correspond to the functions of the messenger (see 2 Kgs 2:11; Sir 48:10-12; commentary on Mal 3:1). "Before the day of the Lord comes, the great and terrible
day" repeats the traditional imagery of that "day" (v. 23b [4:5b]; see Isa 3:5;
Joel 2:11; 3:4 [2:31]).

Verse 3:23b [4:5b] may have been judged an inadequate conclusion of
Malachi. For whatever reason, another verse was appended (v. 24a [4:6a]).
It continues the thought of the first appendix (3:22a [4:4a]) in a chiastic structure whereby "fathers" is the left stroke of the X and "children" is the right
stroke of the X. The verse offers a comment on the purpose of the covenant
law, that is, mutual love among parents and children. The verse concludes
with a traditional warning from the Lord: "Lest I come and strike the land
with doom" (v. 24b [4:6b]).

> Lo, I will send you
>   Elijah, the prophet,
> Before the day of the LORD comes,
>   the great and terrible day.

The verse that concludes Malachi in the New American Bible is not found in the Hebrew text. Commentators propose that rabbis included it in order to formulate an appropriate conclusion, *not* one of doom. They inserted a repetition of verse 23 [4:5], which associates Elijah with the day of the Lord.

Conclusion

The prophet Malachi ministered to the community of Israel at a "trough" period. The process of rebuilding the temple and reconstituting a religious identity had been completed nearly fifty years beforehand. The glorious visions of Haggai and First Zechariah had not been fulfilled. Expectations of a new age related to the cosmopolitan world-view of Alexander the Great had also been disappointing.

The prophet faced a lethargic priesthood and community in which serious cultic, religious, and social abuses were not examined nor judged adequately. How could he revitalize the situation? He would appeal to the one consistent memory of a faithful God of the covenant! His exhortations would give all concerned a sense of continuity with a faded but glorious tradition. Opportunities to meet the same requirements of faithful living in the present would challenge everyone.

The Book of Malachi emerges as an effective text for rousing the hearts of the disenchanted and disappointed. In an age in which nothing spectacular occurred in religious, social, or political arenas to offer temporary distraction or assistance, Malachi offered a clear critique on the status quo. The prophet presents a creative relationship between the Law and the Prophets that can sustain and carry forth the community. The covenant offers a model of integrity between actions and words that is the basis for worship, leadership, and teaching.

The structure of the book is an effective resource for initial evangelization as well as later situations. The disputation style carefully distinguishes between God's exhortations and comments and the questions of the community. The additional responses offer opportunities for clarification and deeper understanding.

The language combines traditional metaphors and new insights in a clear, direct style. The book is not pedantic, dense, or unappealing. The insights often expressed in ironic phrases, questions, and statements breathe a new spirit into traditional material from the Law and the Prophets.

The Book of Malachi is an appropriate text with which to conclude the Twelve Minor Prophets as well as the Old Testament. It is a witness to the mystery of a faithful God who gives individuals and communities what is needed for the present. It is a perennial call to respond to the God who first loved all of creation and continues to transform the cosmos until the blessings promised "on that day" are no longer expectations.

REVIEW AIDS AND DISCUSSION TOPICS

I

Introduction (pages 5–15)

1. Describe how exploring a text of the Bible is like the experience of viewing picture in a photo album for a viewer as well as for a photographer.
2. Why does postexilic prophecy often receive less attention than early prophecy
3. Outline the historical background for Joel, Obadiah, Haggai, Zechariah, an Malachi. Are there similarities for each period?
4. Why was the question of identity important to the exiles returning from Baby lon? How was it related to other religious values?
5. Why were the postexilic prophets associated with apocalyptic writings?

II

THE BOOK OF JOEL

Part One: Joel 1:1–2:17 (pages 16–24)

1. What is the relationship of Part One to a lamentation liturgy? Describe four group: within the community that are called to lamentation (1:5-14).
2. What is the significance of the plague of locusts (1:1-4)?
3. Why is the statement about the *imminent* "day of the Lord" alarming to the com munity (1:15-18)?
4. What is the catastrophe? How is it described (2:1-11)? How does the community respond (2:12-17)?

III

Part Two: Joel 2:18–4:21 [2:18–3:21] (pages 24–32)

1. What is the relationship of Part Two to a lamentation liturgy?
2. How does the Lord reveal compassion for the community (2:18-27)?
3. Which blessing for the community appears most surprising (3:1-5)? Why?
4. Indicate the components that comprise God's judgment on the nations (4:1-17)
5. Contrast God's blessings for the community with the judgment imposed on the nations (4:18-21).
6. What is the contribution of Joel to his community? To future communities of be lievers?

IV

THE BOOK OF OBADIAH

Part One: Obadiah 1-14, 15b (*pages* 33–39)

1. Outline the relationship between Israel and Edom from the period described in Genesis to the period of Herod the Great.

2. Name the dispositions of Edom's heart condemned by God (vv. 2-3).

3. Describe the intensity of Edom's destruction (vv. 4-9).

4. Give the characteristics of Edom's treachery against Judah (vv. 10-14).

V

Part Two: Obadiah 15a, 16-21 (*pages* 39–43)

1. List several points of similarity between the Books of Joel and Obadiah.

2. How is the custom of *lex talionis* operative in the judgment of the nations (v. 16)?

3. Indicate some significant dimensions of the return and restoration of Israel (vv. 17-21).

4. How would you describe the contribution of the Book of Obadiah?

VI

THE BOOK OF HAGGAI

Part One: Haggai 1:1-15a (*pages* 44–50)

1. Describe the function of Zerubbabel and Joshua. What biographical details would give them additional importance in the temple-community?

2. What is the situation in Haggai's period regarding progress on the reconstruction of the temple?

3. How is the attitude of the community toward rebuilding the temple indicated in the first oracle (1:2-11)?

4. Does the comparison between human efforts and results appear important to the development of the first oracle?

VII

Part Two: Haggai 1:15b–2:23 (*pages* 50–57)

1. What is the occasion for the third oracle (1:15b–2:9)?

2. Compare the expectations of the community concerning the rebuilding project with the model of the first temple (2:3).

3. How does the Lord assure the community? What does the editor add to develop the assurance (2:4-5)?

4. Describe the Lord's actions and promise of blessings (2:6-9).

5. Which interpretation regarding the indictment of the temple-community (2:14) do you favor? Why?

6. Discuss the contribution of the Book of Haggai to his community and to subsequent communities of believers.

VIII

THE BOOK OF ZECHARIAH

First Zechariah: 1:1–8:23 (pages 58–88)

1. Which is the most difficult section of First Zechariah to interpret?
2. Why does the prophet refer to the "former prophets"?
3. How do the fourth and fifth visions propose a new model of leadership for the temple-community?
4. Which figure in the new model of authority is preferred, according to the oracles (6:9-15)? What factors need to be considered for your reply?
5. According to chapter 8, how will Jerusalem function in the future? Is there any new revelation here?

IX

Second Zechariah: 9:1–14:21 (pages 89–107)

1. Outline the major differences between First and Second Zechariah.
2. What are the themes developed in Second Zechariah? Do they occur in First Zechariah?
3. How is God's judgment against the enemies of Israel described (9:1b-9)? For Israel (11-10:1)?
4. Describe how the future messiah will restore Israel (10:3b-12).
5. How will Jerusalem be purified (13:2-6)?
6. Explain why chapter 14 is apocalyptic in language and content.

X

THE BOOK OF MALACHI

Introduction: Text and Commentary (pages 108–125)

1. Describe briefly how the six oracles are related to the covenant relationship between God and the community of Israel.
2. What is the relationship of ritual offenses (1:6-14; 3:6-12) to the actions and words of the priests and the people?
3. Do the appendices add new insights to the book? Why or why not?
4. What is the value of the Book of Malachi for faith communities?